KU-559-568

# THE ENGLISH RISING OF 1381

# THE ENGLISH RISING OF 1381

By

R. H. HILTON AND H. FAGAN

LONDON
LAWRENCE AND WISHART
1950

"Serfs are not born; they are serfs by an act of conquest. All men are equal; nobility comes neither from wealth nor birth. A man who earns his bread by carrying a sack on his back has more nobility than a lawless prince."

—Boendale (fourteenth-century Brabantine)

"The rising of the Jacquerie [the French peasants, 1358] was the prelude to the collapse of a regime which had once been necessary and useful, but which had become a crushing burden on the country. The feudal order deserved to die: here is the dossier for the sentence of death."

—Siméon Luce. *La Jacquerie*

# CONTENTS

## *PUBLISHERS' NOTE*

Part I, and Chapter XII of Part II, were written by R. H. Hilton.

Part II, with the exception of Chapter XII, was written by H. Fagan. It is based on his earlier work, *Nine Days That Shook England* (Gollancz, 1938) which has been entirely revised and rewritten for the present edition.

## SOME IMPORTANT DATES

9th and 10th centuries Period of definition of main institutions of European feudalism.

1066 Conquest of England by Norman, Flemish, French and Breton Barons.

1086 Compilation of Domesday Book.

1087 Death of William I (Conqueror). Accession of William II (Rufus).

1100 Death of William II. Accession of Henry I.

1135 Death of Henry I. Accession of Stephen.

1138-53 Intermittent Civil War between supporters of Stephen and of Mathilda (Henry I's daughter).

1154 Death of Stephen. Accession of Henry II.

1189 Death of Henry II. Accession of Richard I, who was only in England for a few months of his reign.

1199 Death of Richard I. Accession of John.

1204 Loss of the Duchy of Normandy by John to the King of France.

1215 Magna Carta.

1216 Death of John. Accession of Henry III.

1258-65 Baronial revolt and civil war.

1272 Death of Henry III. Accession of Edward I. Wars against Wales, France and Scotland.

1307 Death of Edward I. Accession of Edward II.

1327 Deposition and murder of Edward II.

1330 Beginning of Edward III's majority.

| | |
|---|---|
| 1337 | Beginning of Hundred Years' War. |
| 1340 | Government crisis. Removal of clerical ministers. |
| 1349-51 | Black Death. |
| 1349 | Ordinance of Labourers. |
| 1360 | Peace of Brétigny. |
| 1369 | Renewal of War. |
| 1371 | Parliamentary attack on clergy and clerical ministers. |
| 1373 | Unsuccessful expedition of John of Gaunt to France. |
| 1376 | Parliamentary attack on Gaunt—the "Good" Parliament. |
| 1377 | Poll Tax, that is a tax levied on every person above 15 years of age. Death of Edward III. Accession of Richard II (a minor). |
| 1379 | Poll Tax. |
| 1380 | Poll Tax. |
| 1381 | The Rising. |

# INTRODUCTION

The English rising of 1381 was not, as some historians have presented it, an unfortunate interruption in the ordered progress of British history. It was an event of European significance. The fourteenth century was an age of profound social and political crisis such as has always accompanied the collapse of outmoded social systems. It must be remembered that the English rising occurred in the same century as the rising of the peasants of maritime Flanders, as the French Jacquerie and as the class battles in Flemish and other European industrial towns. Almost contemporary with the English rising were the risings of the Ciompi in Florence (1378) and of the weavers of Ghent and Bruges under Philip van Artevelde (1379-82). At the same time the wars in Italy, France and Germany showed that there was as little harmony in the ranks of the rulers of society as there was between rulers and ruled.

Much has been written of the causes and course of the English rising. We venture to offer this further attempt at an explanation for two reasons.

Firstly, we believe that previous accounts have been written by authors who, to a greater or lesser degree, willingly or unconsciously, have been influenced by the bias shown against the rebels by all the sources, literary and official. Recognising the inevitability of class conflict in class-divided societies, we attempt to redress the balance by reconstructing the inadequately recorded motives and aims, not of the oppressors, but of the oppressed.

Secondly, we believe that previous analyses of the crisis which produced the rising—the crisis, in fact, of feudal society[1] as a whole—have been inadequate or incorrect. This is partly because of the method of analysis which has been used, but also because recent research has brought new facts to light which must bring about a reassessment. An attempt has been made, therefore, in the first part of the book to describe the economic and social situation in the fourteenth century on the basis of materials some of which are not available to the general reader. It should be stressed, however, that neither of us has aimed at producing a work of erudition. We have tried to write a book which will present to the British people one part of their own tradition of struggle for popular liberties.

[1] We use the terms "feudal" and "feudalism" differently from many historians. By "feudalism" we mean that type of social organisation in Europe which developed from the ruins of the Roman Empire and which persisted, though with many changes of form, until the sixteenth and seventeenth centuries, when capitalism was born. With us, therefore, the term does not denote merely the holding of land for military service or the decentralisation of public authority or any other temporary feature of the period.

# *Part One*

## *THE PREPARATION FOR THE RISING*

CHAPTER ONE

# FEUDAL SOCIETY: LORDS AND PEASANTS

IN THE summer of 1381 England was shaken from top to bottom by the Great Revolt: this was at once a symptom and cause of the collapse of a decaying order of society.

The revolt was no sudden or chance uprising but the outcome of a number of complicated and inter-related antagonisms. Basic to these was the conflict between feudal lord and serf. Medieval politics cannot be understood without a knowledge of the details, and of the economic and social consequences, of this conflict. But feudal society was complex and contained relics of the older orders of society from which it had evolved—such as the slave society of ancient Rome and the tribal economy of the primitive Germans. Moreover, not only did the different societies of Europe develop at uneven rates, but they interacted one upon another. Growing within this system, in as yet embryonic form, were the newer forms of production and association which, in the centuries following, were to burst it asunder and transform first Europe and then the world.

In analysing the events of 1381, and the crisis of feudal society which the revolt laid bare, it will also be seen that the superstructure of ideas and institutions which had evolved from the mode of production in this society—the political and legal institutions, the religious and social organisations, the political theories and social ideals of the different classes—all played their part in the struggle and determined the historic shape which it took.

The medieval serf was the producer who bore on his back all the unproductive elements of society—nobles, ecclesiastics, merchants. The keystone of feudal society is found in the social relations between the serfs and the landowners, for production then was overwhelmingly agricultural or pastoral. The serf was the head of a peasant family, almost invariably associated with other peasant families in a village or hamlet community. The vast majority of peasant families had their own plots of arable land in the village, supplemented by communal grazing rights and access to communal woodland. It was from these holdings that the peasant family gained its livelihood and the means for carrying on production from year to year. But by the time that the feudal regime was established, peasant farming had a long history behind it, dating back to the Neolithic age some 3,000 years before our era. Skills and techniques had been developed so that the peasant communities produced a considerable amount more than they needed for their bare living. Part of this surplus had been used for ages past to support craftsmen, traders and the aristocracies of both Celtic and Teutonic tribal kingdoms. Under feudalism a large part of it went to support the nobility.

The feudal ruling class was a landowning class which laid claim not only to the ownership of its own private demesnes (the home farms under the immediate control of bailiffs), but also of all the peasant holdings and the common woods and pastures of the peasant village or hamlet communities. At this stage of social development, however, it was obliged to permit the peasant communities to continue in *possession,* though not in *ownership,* of their lands. Population was scarce, and a very small proportion of what was produced went to the market. This made the exploitation of wage-labour on any significant scale by the lords impossible. So they lived by taking away the peasant producer's surplus in the form of rent. Since the peasant had his own means of producing his family's livelihood, the lords had to take the rent away from the peasant through the undisguised exercise of force. The appropriation was naked and unashamed. This is why the great majority of medieval peasants were serfs, that is legally unfree, though their effective possession of their own land gave them a very different status from the chattel slaves of ancient society.

The lord took the rent from the peasant in many different ways. It might be a fixed or variable proportion of the products of the peasant holding—grain, dairy produce, stock. It might be the actual surplus labour of the peasant—surplus that is to the labour done on his own holding for his own and his family's subsistence. In this case the lord would use this surplus labour on his own demesne or home farm. At a later stage, when the production of commodities for the market was fairly advanced, and when consequently there was more money in circulation, labour services and rents in kind were given a cash value and a money rent was paid in their stead. This process of conversion was known as "commutation", and was an important stage in the partial emancipation of the richer peasants from landlord control. But its importance must not be misunderstood. Money rent was still a "feudal" rent representing the forcibly extracted surplus of the peasant producer. It is in no way comparable to the rent paid in a capitalist society to a landlord. The rent paid by the medieval peasant to his lord must be looked at as the principal aspect of the social relationship between an exploiting and exploited class, the lord and serf, the two main classes of feudal society.

The coercive apparatus by which this exploitation was assured varied considerably from place to place and from period to period. Early feudalism knew no developed central state machine, acting on behalf of the ruling class as a whole. Coercion was decentralised. The lords had their own local courts through which they ruled their own estates. The central king's court, from which eventually developed the main central state organs of the whole ruling class, was at first regarded as being but a larger and more important administrative centre of a private estate. Although the monarchies from the thirteenth to the fifteenth centuries achieved a considerable centralisation of state power, there were in both France and England many remnants of the local jurisdictions which had arisen in the tenth, eleventh and twelfth centuries.

What were the other strata in feudal society? First, the peasant population was not subordinated to a uniform level of servility. According to a whole variety of historical and geographical circumstances there were to be found, from district to district, greater and lesser degrees of freedom from exploitation. There were also variations in the amount of land the peasants held—variations not always coinciding with variations in freedom of status. Then there had been, since Anglo-Saxon times, market centres which slowly grew into trading and industrial towns. The trading was mostly the local exchange of agricultural produce and those few things needed in peasant communities which they could not produce themselves. Only in a few towns, and more especially London, were imported commodities, such as wines and spices, bought and sold. Industry was based on the production of the individual master craftsmen, the majority of whom sold in the front of their shops, or on the town market, that which they made in the back of their shops. The unit of production was small and did not normally comprise more than the master craftsman and one or two apprentices or journeymen (fully trained craftsmen who had not yet set up on their own). Only in one or two industries, notably cloth-making, where the market was national—even international—rather than local, were the wealthy merchants beginning to subordinate to themselves a large number of craftsmen. In these industries they interposed themselves between producers and consumers as middlemen, rather than as organisers of production.

The craftsmen of the towns were organised in gilds which enrolled as members masters, journeymen and apprentices. This practice lasted until a real class cleavage developed between masters and journeymen, that is when journeymen no longer had any hope of becoming masters, as the masters themselves were imposing such restrictions, financial and other, on their entry into the gilds that the possibility of setting up independently as masters became ever more remote. Then the journeymen attempted to set up their own organisations, attempts which were stringently suppressed or side-tracked by being brought under the control of the masters' organisations. This movement was beginning in the fourteenth century and did not become fully significant for another century. The main conflict was between the wealthy merchants' gilds which attempted to monopolise the sale of finished goods, and the craftsmen's gilds which tried to protect the producers from the price-fixing and output demands of the merchants. The acuteness of these struggles varied according to the degree of urban development. The struggles in London, as will be seen below, were more complex than those in the smaller towns which catered principally for a local market.

At the other end of the social scale were the lords, and here too were great variations of wealth and power. The owners of the biggest estates—earls, barons, bishops, abbots, priors—had landed interests stretching over many counties. The prior and monks of the Cathedral Chapter of Canterbury were supported by an estate of some fifty manors in Kent, the Thames Valley and East Anglia, and had flocks of fourteen thousand sheep. The income from this estate, in the money of the end of the thirteenth century, was about £2,500, and this was in the upper division of baronial incomes. There were however a few—perhaps half a dozen—such as the Earl of Cornwall, the Earl of Gloucester or the Earl of Norfolk, who, at the same period, had incomes of more than £3,000 or £4,000 from their estates.

These great estate owners, lay and ecclesiastical, were the social intimates of the king, helping him to shape his policy. Their class interests were fundamentally identical with his, however much conflict of immediate personal or political interest might divide them among themselves or from him. The ruling class of feudal society was no more exempt from internal conflicts than other ruling classes before or since. When these divisions occurred, many of the lesser barons tended to be drawn in on one side or another. Most of them were involved for many reasons with one or more of the great magnates. Some were related to them by marriage, others might hold most of their land from one great baron, others might be drawn into supporting a powerful magnate, even in the absence of a landlord-tenant relationship, because of the magnate's overwhelming local influence. It should also be stressed that when these conflicts within the nobility became national rather than local, the king himself might become involved, giving one of the parties the appearance of a royalist, the other of an opposition party. This is not to say that English kings were mere ciphers. Their own interests were extremely powerful, but we must not imagine them isolated from their class, whether its prevailing internal social relations were harmonious or discordant.

The knights occupied the lowest place in the social scale of the feudal rulers. Originally owing military service to the king's host as part of the quota of mounted men due from the barons, and receiving in return one or two manors, they were by no means an unimportant element in medieval society. It was they who were responsible for the routine administration of the central government's local organs, and they are of great significance economically in the transition to capitalist society. They, too, were not undifferentiated as far as income or influence was concerned. Some might only be getting £20 or £30 a year from one small manor, not much more than some wealthy freeholders. Others would have accumulated estates worth four or five times that amount, and be merging into the lesser baronage. But their role must not be overestimated, for politically they remained dependent on the baronage until the sixteenth and seventeenth centuries. Hence in surveying those conditions in fourteenth century England which produced the revolt of 1381, we have to consider first the economic and social conditions that were shaped by the great estates of the lay and ecclesiastical baronage.

By no means the whole of England was involved in the economy of the great estate. Even in those regions of the South and South East where the great estates predominated, there were many smaller lords who owned from one to five manors. There were also free tenants who only owed some small service or rent in one form or another for their holdings and were thus comparatively free from feudal exploitation. Many of them were, nevertheless, only smallholders who, in order to live, had to sell their labour at disadvantageous terms to make up the labour requirements of the big estates at harvest-time. In the North and North-West the organisation of the big estate was much looser than in the South. Pre-feudal conditions still persisted in those parts of the country which were not advanced enough for anything but a sheep and cattle grazing economy. Even where there were great sheep flocks whose wool was exported abroad there was less need for servile labour than in the farming areas which produced grain and other crops.

But the great estate dominated the economic structure, and

in many regions determined the life of all the inhabitants. The principal unit of the estate was the manor which, whatever its local variations, generally consisted of a home farm or *demesne,* with anything from 100 to 500 acres of arable land; the much smaller holdings of the free and servile peasant tenants, varying from ten to thirty acres apart from the acre plots of smallholders or cottagers; and the woods, wastes and pastures which were held in common by the village community. Often the manor coincided in extent with the village, sometimes the village was divided up into two or more manors, and sometimes a manor included several villages and hamlets. The manor was supervised by a lord's bailiff who had under him a peasant reeve (analogous to a foreman). The labour on the demesne was mainly supplied by the peasants and their families, who owed a variety of unpaid services, such as ploughing, reaping, carting, as part of their rent. This work was supplemented by the work of permanent hired men, and casual labour at harvest and other peak periods. The bailiff or reeve was responsible for getting the maximum output from the demesne, for collecting rents in money and kind, for disciplining and fining the tenants in the manor court (under the supervision of a higher official, the steward), and for selling surplus produce at the best prices on the local market. The whole estate was organised by an elaborate hierarchy of officials—receivers, auditors, stewards, bailiffs, backed up by the lord's personal council of local gentry, lawyers and land agents. It was a very expensive organisation which worked well when profits were easy to come by.

The thirteenth and early fourteenth centuries in England,[1] saw the estate at its most active as a vigorously working economic and social unit. As a part of this activity the estate owners began to make careful surveys of landed

[1] In France and Western Germany the great estates had had their day more than a century earlier.

property, to keep annual accounts and records of manorial courts. This period was the last phase of an era of the expansion of the social order which had been continuous since about the middle of the eleventh century. The characteristics of this phase of our history were a steady increase in population, in the volume of agricultural production, of handicraft industry and of both national and international commerce. The price of corn increased by 25 per cent in the first half of the thirteenth century and by 50 per cent in the second half. On one large typical estate in Southern England agricultural production increased by 150 per cent during the century, and the amount of produce sold on the market (compared with that consumed within the estate) increased by 44 per cent.

In a society based on the exploitation of a vast peasant majority by a small class of landowners, it was natural that the fruit of this expansion should be enjoyed primarily by the landlords, and to a much lesser degree by intermediate strata of society (such as the free peasantry or even richer serfs). In order to profit from the rising prices of grain and stock the lords increased the land under cultivation by clearing forests and marshes. They intensified their exploitation of the peasantry by demanding extra forced labour services from them. And where the limit to such demands was reached they attempted still further to appropriate to themselves the produce of the labour of the serf and his family in the shape of higher rents both in money and in kind.

In many ways the great estate owners during this boom period showed gifts of organisation and initiative which are reminiscent of the economic "virtues" of the entrepreneurs of early industrial capitalism. No economy was too small if it increased profits, nor was any oppression left untried from motives of Christian charity. The most efficient landlords were in fact the great monasteries. The Abbey of Ramsay in the eastern counties was unsurpassed in its pressure to increase the surplus extracted from its free and servile tenantry. The Abbey of St. Peter's, Gloucester, has left us in its *Scriptum Quoddam* a set of rules for estate administration, which the most ruthless Calvinist exponent of economic individualism could scarcely improve, as far as minute attention to details of profit and loss is concerned.

However, in spite of the extra land taken into cultivation, in spite of some attention to agricultural improvements such as the use of manure and marl, the increased production was largely the fruit of increased exploitation and oppression as well as of rationalised estate administration. There were no basic improvements in the technique of production. There was, for instance, no general increase in the average yield per acre of grain; increased production resulted rather from an increase in the area under crops. There were no fundamental improvements in stock-breeding comparable in any way to those of the eighteenth century. The landowning class in its search for profit could do no more in the long run than overstrain the organisation at its disposal, because it was unable to increase productivity enough to meet the ever growing demands of war, taxation, and its own expanding standard of living.

One of the symptoms of the economic decline of the fourteenth and fifteenth centuries is a stagnation or even a drop in agricultural prices, the consequence of a shrinking market. This was in fact but a symptom of the gradual stagnation of a mode of production which had been pushed to the breaking point of its productive resources but which was technically unable to expand further, and which was therefore unable to support more than a certain population. At the same time the prices of commodities which entered into agricultural costs rose. This "price scissors" was not a new phenomenon. But these conditions were intensified in the fourteenth century, and the overhead expenses of the top-heavy feudal estate made the crisis sharper.

Part of this crisis of the fourteenth century economy was a shortage both of serfs and "free" agricultural labour. Over-population relative to the means of subsistence had increased during the thirteenth century and this meant widespread malnutrition. Hence failures of crops caused famine, and brought out the innumerable plagues and diseases which dogged the heels of medieval societies. The Black Death was but one of these outbreaks—not a visitation from heaven but the consequence of oppression and poverty. It considerably aggravated the developing population shortages, since in many districts it destroyed between a third and a half of the working population.

The lords of wide estates found therefore that the produce of the demesne lands was more difficult to sell, and that the servile or wage labour available was not only shrinking in quantity, but becoming less willing to be exploited. The only practical course open was to rid themselves of an encumbrance; to lease out their demesne lands, and to rely for their incomes, not primarily on the sale of their agricultural products but on tenants' rents from the demesnes. Servile labour was therefore no longer required to the same extent, so that ploughing services and the like were "commuted" for a money payment. Instead of the obligation to provide a man's labour on the demesne every other day of the week, the serf found that he had to pay the money value of that labour. This was not necessarily an advantage to him, if his holding produced but a small marketable surplus, but for the richer peasant, who was already producing for the market, it was a welcome opportunity to devote all the labour resources of his family, even sometimes of hired labour, to his own personal holding.

The process by which the lords shed the expenses of a working estate and became "rentiers" was an uneven one.

It appears to have begun earliest in those parts of England where opportunities of producing for the market were least, that is in the North and West. Southern and South-eastern England was a land of towns, busy seaports, and country industries. Consequently, such estates as were already organised to serve the urban (even the foreign) market, kept their old organisation as much as a century longer than the smaller or more remote estates. The manor demesnes of the Bishop of Winchester, for instance, mostly in the South and the Thames Valley, were not being leased out until the fifteenth century, while in some places the commutation movement can be found before the middle of the fourteenth century. The consequence of this unevenness of development was the co-existence, often in the same region, of peasants subject to very differing conditions of exploitation according to the economic policy of their feudal lords. This was an important cause of peasant discontent.

Furthermore, although the ultimate solution of the difficulties which feudal landowners eventually adopted was an abandonment of production, other expedients were tried which deepened the crisis. Important though servile labour was, wage labour also had always played some part in the manorial economy. It even increased in importance as the serf labour of tenants became less available. In particular wage labour was of great importance for the lesser nobility who had always had to rely less on servile tenants than on the paid labour of cottagers and the like. The Black Death resulted in a sharp rise both in prices and wages, partly because of the diminished supply of labour, partly owing to a vast increase in the ratio of money to goods and services. The increased wages demanded by agricultural labourers was a natural reaction to a situation in which the labourers found themselves with greatly increased bargaining powers as against employers. But the mere figures of wages paid after the Black Death do not give any real idea of the chaos of the labour situation in those years. For a time the normal forms of exploitation seemed to be in the process of dissolution. Serfs left the holdings to which they were legally bound and quitted the manor to compete for work with the free smallholders and the landless labourers in both town and country. Consequently both wage labour and serf labour, reduced by between a third and a half by this Plague, was even then practically impossible for individual manorial lords or estate overseers to control. An extraordinary situation was arising from this extreme shortage and uncontrollability of labour—a sort of banditry in which the precious commodity sought by the bandits was not gold or jewels, but labour power. The public records reveal many cases (and only a fraction therefore of the unrecorded total) of complaints by weaker members of the landowning classes, especially, for example, the smaller religious houses, that neighbouring lords were forcibly abducting their serfs. The serfs themselves in some cases were not unwilling conspirators, as for instance when they could come under the rule of a comparatively lax absentee landlord, such as the Crown, instead of that of a former master, such as a grasping monastic corporation.

To remedy this dangerous situation in the absence of Parliament, the authorities in June, 1349, eleven months after the arrival of the Black Death, issued an Ordinance, commonly called the Ordinance of Labourers. This Ordinance was elaborated in a number of subsequent Parliamentary Statutes. The Ordinance and Statutes were immediately enforced by practical administrative measures which were made possible by the growth of the central state apparatus since the thirteenth century and which themselves served to extend the scope of that apparatus. Their implementation was an important step in the process by which the state, representing the interests of the ruling class as a whole, took over tasks which individual nobles and gentry were unable to do locally with such private powers of jurisdiction as they inherited from an earlier age of feudal society. This general aspect of the labour legislation of the period is important in explaining why the rebels in 1381 almost always chose official representatives of the central state power as object lessons in the administration of popular justice.

The aims of the Ordinance and the subsequent Statutes were simple. All able-bodied men and women under sixty who did not own enough land to occupy them full time were to accept any work offered to them either at the wage rates prevailing in 1347, or at certain rates fixed for named occupations. The only restriction to this clause was that their lords were to have the first refusal of their services. Contracts by the day were forbidden, only contracts for six-monthly or yearly periods (or longer) being legal. In the interpretation of the Statute by the courts no written contract was considered necessary. The lord's word was always taken as a definition of the terms of the contract. Lord's officials and local state officials had the right to put into stocks those who would not take this compulsory service under the conditions laid down. In addition bodies of justices, chosen from amongst the local nobility and gentry of the counties, were appointed to try at quarter sessions delinquents under the Statute, and to fine or imprison as the case should merit. Fining was of course more frequent than imprisonment, since imprisonment defeated the objects of the Statutes—the augmentation and maintenance of the labour force. Fining furthermore was profitable, and for six years during the first decade after the Plague the profits of the quarter sessions went to lighten the taxation assessments in the districts where the offences against the Statute were committed. The gentry in general, therefore, as the principal taxpayers, had a double incentive to operate the laws as efficiently and as vigorously as possible.

The justices in particular also had an interest in keeping the pot boiling, for their salaries were paid out of the fines. In three years, the workers contributed by fines about £10,000 to the tax relief of the rich, and in some places the fines exceeded the total tax payable.

Medieval statutes were more often than not pious wishes on paper, but it has been proved conclusively that if any statutes could humanly be operated in their fullness they were the Statutes of Labourers. For they were put into operation in the interests of an exploiting class by leading members of that class at the time of its great crisis. In only one feature did they seem to "fail"—the clause of the Ordinance to keep prices to a "reasonable" level does not seem to have been enforced as rigorously as the wages clause. Who was to say what was a "reasonable" level? But the level of wages was not left to interpretation. The maximum amount to be paid was laid down with precision, but the minimum was not mentioned. In every county the quarter sessions worked with zeal—and, to a certain extent, with success, as the figures of the fines levied suggest. The central courts, too, of Common Pleas and King's Bench were working equally hard in the enforcement of the Statutes. It has been calculated that between 1349 and 1377 they must have considered something like 9,000 cases and, in almost every case for which there is evidence, the jury's verdict or the court's judgment was in favour of the employer as against the employee.

The effect of the enforcement of the Statutes of Labourers on its victims need not be imagined. The proof of the resistance of the labourers to the attempts to control their wages is in the continued need for the gentry to operate the law in its utmost vigour decade after decade. It is also in the growing tide of revolt as revealed by the number of armed attacks which were organised on the justices empowered to operate the Statutes. The peasantry was beginning to extend its political horizons as it broadened its resentment from the well-known local oppressor, the manorial lord, or his bailiff, to the representative of repression as an organised system, the state power. Furthermore the operation of the Statutes had a probably unlooked-for result in extending the social basis of opposition to the Government to a group which might, at first thoughts, have been thought to favour their provisions.

This attempt to render the "free" labour force immobile did not only enrage the agricultural labourers and artisans whose wages were kept down to a starvation level. It also operated against the interests of many employers of labour. The nobility who had considerable local control over the labour supply, by virtue of their political power and their rights of private jurisdiction, also still had access to an appreciable amount of servile labour. It was to their advantage to devise a method by which their supplementary labour supply should be assured at a low price. What they were in fact aiming to do was to eliminate the consequence of competition for available wage labour. The competitors of the nobility were very largely the richer peasants, who in the latter part of the fourteenth century were beginning to employ a considerable amount of wage labour. They, no doubt in common with some of the lesser gentry, had no means of exercising compulsion to get their fields cultivated. Their only resource was to offer high wages. The enforcement of the Statute was not to their advantage, for its effect—certainly its intention—was to place control of the labour supply in the hands of the local nobility. This was probably one amongst many causes for that antagonism of the richer peasantry to the government which brought many of them into the leadership of the revolt of 1381.

The process by which the peasantry as a class became differentiated into rich, poor and landless peasants was one which has often been repeated where commodity production disintegrates a static feudal community.[1] Even in the twelfth and thirteenth centuries, every village had its rich and its poor. The typical class division in that earlier period was however of a different character from that which resulted from the changes in society during and after the fourteenth century. In the earlier village the majority of the shares in the village lands (the lord's demesne apart) were held by a class of "yardlanders" or "half yardlanders", the backbone of the community. The yardland varied considerably from place to place, usually between twenty and thirty acres. But within the village the holdings of the yardlanders were remarkably equal in size. This was due to the absence of a market in land, resulting partly from the small amount of production for the market and partly from the lord's control of the transfer of land, which he restricted so as to maintain the original area of the service-rendering holding. Below the yardlanders were a number of smallholders, some free, some servile in legal status. Some of these had an acre or two in the common fields, some only a cottage and squatting rights on the waste. These cottagers were the original reserve of wage labour.

The development of commodity production, the agrarian crisis, famine, plague, and the declining interest of the lord in maintaining the integrity of holdings so as to ensure the supply of services, resulted in a considerable change in the classes of peasants in the typical village. By the end of the fourteenth century an upper class of peasants had made its appearance. Four or five families in the village were now cultivating sixty or a hundred acres of arable land, and tending several hundred head of live stock. Some of the yardlanders still survived, but at the other end of the scale were the victims of the process of accumulation—an impor-

[1] Lenin's book, *The Development of Capitalism in Russia,* describes the same process in nineteenth-century Russia. The resemblance to developments in fourteenth-century England is most marked.

tant (if still small) group of landless labourers.

Undoubtedly the principal reason for this development was the increasing participation of peasants in the production of agricultural commodities to sell in local markets. This alone, however, cannot explain why the fourteenth century should show a speeding-up of the process. Generally speaking, production for the market slackened during the period. This has been mentioned in writing of the crisis of the nobility. If many of the nobility went bankrupt, so did many of the peasants, who had less reserves to fall back on. But the conditions of agrarian crisis are like those of increased production for the market, favourable to the sort of differentiation to which reference has already been made. As the land of peasants, bankrupt or dead from plague, came into the manorial land-market, the lord was incapable of absorbing it into his own holding, his demesne. He was in fact trying to get rid of the demesne lands. Hence a considerable quantity of land at cheap rents, both from the lapsed lands of impoverished peasants, and from the lord's demesne, was made available. The peasant who survived took it over. Such a peasant was very often the village reeve, who as a lord's official had enjoyed special advantages and privileges. He was often also the village usurer—a familiar figure in primitive peasant communities. It was men like these who were competing with the nobility for wage labour, and against whose competition the Statute of Labourers was invoked.

But if the upper peasants were able to take advantage of the economic embarrassments of both nobles and poorer peasants, they still remained socially and politically a subject group in society. In a thousand and one ways the institutions of feudal society hampered the would-be producer for the market. He still lived within the framework of the manor, every one of the regulations of which was designed, somehow or other, to appropriate the surplus labour or the surplus product of the peasant producer. Unless the lord had chosen to commute labour services, the peasant producer (however rich he might be) could be forced to provide a man to work three or four days a week on the lord's demesne, besides extra ploughing, harrowing, mowing, reaping and carting. In addition to a money rent he might have to give ancient customary dues in kind, such as eggs at Easter or hens at Christmas. Together with the other villagers, he had to pay his lord an annual private tax or "tallage". He might be forced to grind his corn at the lord's mill, bake his bread at the lord's bakery, brew his beer at the lord's brewery—all of course for a payment. If his son sought employment outside the manor he paid for the privilege, annually. He had to get permission (and pay a fine) for the son to go to school, and to pay a fine to marry off his daughters. If he himself brought in hired labour from outside the manor the lord was paid for the privilege, annually. If he wished to sell any of his livestock he had to get, and pay for, the lord's licence. If, in these conditions, he managed to accumulate any wealth, the lord saw to it that a good proportion was taken off his widow and heir on his death. The lord took his best beast (at least) as "heriot", and the church, not content with having taken tithes from him during his life, took the second-best beast as "mortuary". The heir could only succeed to the tenement on payment of an entry fine, which was sometimes fixed at one year's rent, but was often higher. A serf in Wiltshire in the early fifteenth century, through a combination of agriculture and domestic manufacture of cloth, had managed to accumulate possessions valued by the lord of the manor at nearly £2,000. This was probably an overestimate, but nevertheless the heir was mulcted of £140 by the lord before he succeeded to his father's property.

The rich peasant, chafing at these feudal restrictions on his economic enterprise, was as revolutionary a figure as the poor or landless peasant oppressed by the Statute of Labourers, and by onerous rents and services. The programme of demands put forward by the united peasantry at Mile End on June 14, 1381 (p. 129-30), represented the interests of all sections, temporarily united in one rebellious upsurge. But also the growing divisions within the peasantry, the one section capitalist farmers in embryo, the other rural proletariat, reflected themselves in the demands. These divisions, as well as the very conditions of the peasant economy, made them, as a class, unable to develop that ultimate unity of purpose so necessary to defeat a ruling class.

The irksome life of the peasants and the growing inability of the lords to make their system work were such as to turn the peasants towards revolt in order to remedy their conditions. It was not only the immediate circumstances which turned the peasants' thoughts towards armed rebellion. Behind the English peasantry lay the experience of at least a century and a half of local struggles, sometimes successful, but more often defeated by a combination of lord and central government. The action of the men of Kent and East Anglia was the fruit of countless isolated village struggles of peasant communities against feudal order, even of the individual serf against his lord. It was a struggle which we can trace in the written record back at least to the beginning of the thirteenth century. It was a struggle around the fundamental class issue of feudal society—who was to enjoy the fruit of the peasants' toil?

The earliest known cases of resistance in the thirteenth century in opposition to a movement to increase rent were, as should be expected, the resistance of individuals. On many manors the lords were attempting to increase the labour services and other forms of rent. Those few peasants of indisputably free legal status were in a position to offer resistance to rent increases. They were entitled to fight the case in the royal courts, and a free rent established by custom was hard to challenge in a society where the whole atmosphere was one of respect for the established order. The indisputably unfree peasant had no redress against his lord in the royal courts, and he was therefore at the lord's mercy in the manorial court—unless he could organise effective collective resistance. But by no means all peasants admitted that they *were* indisputably unfree, so that the struggle for rent in its first phase appears as the struggle to define status. The lords attempted to show that their tenants were legally unfree and could therefore be exploited "at will": the peasants attempted to prove that they were legally free, or that other legal rights restricted their rent to a fixed level.

There were, therefore, innumerable cases in the royal courts of the early thirteenth century in which peasant pedigrees that were long enough to put "ancient" families to shame were produced, to determine whether such and such an individual was of servile descent or not. A typical example of such cases is recorded in his notebook by the famous thirteenth century lawyer, Bracton. In 1224 the Abbot of Battle (near Hastings, Sussex) was apparently trying to double the services of two peasants in the village of Crowmarsh, Oxfordshire. These two, through the voice of one of them, claimed to be free men, whose rents should not therefore be increased. So the Abbot produced a second cousin of his peasant opponent who was proved to be unfree. This was the main factor which gave the Abbot the victory, but in addition he showed that the two men also did villein works and services as did the others in the village who were acknowledged by all to be true villeins, and to whose exploitation there was therefore no legal limit.

This and many other similar cases resulted in the final condemnation to villeinage and to unrestricted exploitation of many a peasant in many a manor throughout England. We only know of such cases because they penetrated through to the royal courts. Many more sporadic protests must have been stifled in the manor court. The movement of protest through legal channels did not, however, stop at the refusal by individuals to acquiesce in individual burdens. Sometimes the peasants tried to prove that they were all free, as those of Stoughton in Leicestershire did in 1279. Leicestershire was a country which had been thickly settled by Danes after their invasions of Britain. These Scandinavian peoples, nearer to tribal society than the Anglo-Saxons amongst whom they settled, created a tradition of peasant freedom in Eastern England. So the men—and women—of Stoughton claimed to be free "sokemen", paying only a money rent to the Abbot of Leicester, with occasional attendance at his court. But the Abbot was more powerful in the king's court than the peasants and was able to bring witnesses to swear to his tenants' servility. The king's justices were always prepared to protect the interests of those who could prove their freedom beyond any shadow of doubt, for freemen were useful, even vital elements in local administration. But the justices were also serf-exploiting landlords, and so was the king. Between lord and serf they could not interfere.

It is not, however, from these scattered though increasingly frequent references in the records of the central government that we get the most vivid impression of the elements of social revolt boiling up under the deceptively placid surface of the English country villages. The records of the manorial courts are the truest reflection of the day-to-day struggle of the serfs against feudal exploitation. This struggle took many forms—flight from the manor to the nearest town where freedom could be obtained (if the serf remained uncaught after a year and a day), non-payment of money rent or rent in kind, scamped performance of labour services, and, most important, deliberate withdrawal of labour services owed on the lord's demesne land. The more manorial court rolls come to light, the more significant does this constant battle for feudal rent appear. It is a movement that is not easy to express statistically. It appears most vividly through actual entries in the court rolls themselves. An indication of the scale of this local movement can be quoted from the evidence of the Court Rolls of the Huntingdonshire Abbey of Ramsay. During the course of twenty-one court sessions held in various Abbey manors in the last quarter of the thirteenth century there were no fewer than 146 convictions for deliberate non-performance of labour services. Nor were these only cases of individuals who did not turn up, for instance, to the reaping at the bailiff's summons. In many cases what was involved was a mass withdrawal of services, as for instance at Cranfield in February 1294 when twenty-six peasants were fined for staying away from the lord's ploughing, or at Houghton in 1308 when sixteen peasants were fined because they went off after dinner and ploughed their own land when they should have ploughed the lord's land. It was this daily resistance which was the preparation for the village revolt, just as the village revolts, going on for over a century, were the preparation for the great revolt of 1381.

From the end of the thirteenth century onwards there is clearly a rising tide of stubborn opposition revealing itself from time to time in the records of the central government, when its intervention to strengthen the hand of the lord was called for. In 1299 for instance, the Prior of St. Stephen's, Hempton, called for governmental assistance to help him to distrain[1] his villeins of Worsted to perform their due and accustomed services. The sheriff of Norfolk ordered the king's common minister for the execution of writs to go down to Worsted to give this help to the Prior. This unfortunate

1 "Distraint" was a process by which a man's necessary plough-oxen or other implements, commodities, etc., were taken from him to force him to do service, pay rent, etc.

official was set upon and assaulted by sixty-six persons, all of whom he names in the accusation against the men of Worsted. Such "conspiracy" to refuse service and to resist their enforcement becomes a regular occurrence in the countryside. Common action is also often found arising not so much from premeditated plans for joint denial of services, but from solidarity with individual victims of manorial oppression. Thus in 1338 the Prior of Tynemouth's officials were leading off to prison a bondman of his manor of Elstwick for the crime of trespassing on the Prior's land with his beasts. Led by a man from Newcastle a group of fellow-serfs rescued the bondman, released his beasts from pound, assaulted the Prior's officials and monks, and took over the manor of Elstwick so that the Prior's servants could collect no rents there. Another of many similar recorded cases occurred in 1349 in Cambridgeshire. The Countess of Pembroke's officials had taken two of her bondmen into custody for disobedience and rebellion. They were on their way to be "chastised in the usual manner" when they were rescued by their friends—a rescue which involved apparently some physical damage to the Countess's officials.

Such was the relationship between the two main classes of English society when the Black Death, the dislocation of economy and the intensification of exploitation through the operation of the Statute of Labourers aggravated an already explosive situation. Although the richer peasants had not hitherto appeared as the leaders of local resistance (official records do not record such detail) in the thirty years before the outbreak of the Great Revolt they had good reason to associate with—and because of their social position in the village even to lead—the movement of resistance to the landlords. The events of 1381, especially in East Anglia, show that by that date some of the richer peasants had begun to take the lead in the fight against their rulers.

CHAPTER TWO

# ENGLISH POLITICS ON THE EVE OF THE RISING

WHILST, IN introducing an account of the rising, it is necessary to give first consideration to the conditions of the peasants as the main exploited class, this does not mean that the other elements in feudal society were of negligible importance. There were sharp economic and political discontents and clashes in the towns as well as in the countryside. Furthermore the changes in the economy already outlined could not have occurred without the development of trade and industry, leading to a greater circulation of money and an increase in the number of consumers who did not themselves produce foodstuffs.

As a matter of fact town populations probably declined rather than rose in the fourteenth and fifteenth centuries—with certain exceptions (of which London and Bristol are the most important). This was part of the general decline in population, but was also in part due to the shift of an important section of the industrial population to the countryside—the clothworkers. But because of their changed location they did not make the less demand for foodstuffs from the agricultural population.

The most important developments in English industry and commerce during the fourteenth century were the rapid growth of the cloth industry, the beginnings of its transfer from town to country, the development of merchant oligarchies in the towns, especially London, and the decay of the gild system.

In thirteenth-century England, industries (in so far as they were not village or manorial crafts producing for village consumption) were for the most part serving a regional market. Only certain towns were producing small quantities of high-grade cloth for the national and European market. Consequently the typical producer, whether of saddles, shoes, cloth, or metal goods, was a town craftsman making and retailing his own goods in one establishment. His interests —restriction of output, limitation of competition, maintenance of prices—were safeguarded by the craft gild to which he belonged. The gild normally had exclusive supervision of supply of material, manufacture, and the sale of the product. So long as the market remained restricted this pattern did not change. True, the craftsmen did have grievances. Even at the beginning of the thirteenth century, town politics were monopolised by merchants rather than by craftsmen, but the line of division was not hard and fast. Markets expanded during the course of the century, and by the fourteenth century the division between producers—craftsmen—and merchants who were only interested in selling the product had become much sharper. It was all the sharper in those towns and those industries where trade had grown, where mercantile profits were greater and where, as a consequence, merchants had gone further in organising a monopoly for themselves in the retail sale of the commodity. Of these the Drapers' Companies are the best example, since cloth manufacture was the most flourishing industry. The London drapers forced the cloth-working craftsmen to sell their products to them alone and in so obtaining a monopoly in the retail cloth trade were able to reap huge profits by charging monopoly prices to their customers and paying minimum prices to the cloth-worker craftsmen.

Merchant monopoly existed side by side with craft monopoly, and was hostile to it. In the cloth industry the association of craftsmen in the gild opposed the expansion of production, and the admission of new master-craftsmen. On the other hand although the merchants wished to break down this exclusiveness it was only to subordinate the craftsmen to themselves almost in a wage-earner relationship. Hence both journeymen, propertyless wage-earners wanting to rise in the world, and master craftsmen, ambitious to avoid both gild jealousy and draper domination, migrated to country districts such as Essex, Kent, Suffolk and Wiltshire. But although, by the time of the rising, these migrants were profoundly modifying the social structure of the villages in which they had settled, the fierce faction fights between gilds, craftsmen, journeymen, and merchants did not cease in the towns.

It so happens that the political movement in three of the most important towns during the rising, St. Albans, Bury St. Edmunds and Cambridge, more resembled the movement of the richer peasants than it did the class struggles in the bigger towns. The first two towns were dominated by the Abbeys in whose demesnes they stood and their struggle was simply for freedom of industry and trade against feudal restrictions. The Abbeys tried to treat their towns as though they were rural manors, and their burgesses serfs. The movement at Cambridge was similar, for it was directed against a clerical institution, the University, which dominated the town market in its own interests. On the other hand, it would appear that the main issue in towns such as Canterbury and Winchester was that of crafts versus merchant oligarchies, each wishing to control the government of the town.

But the politics of the city of London, most important of all, were exceptionally complex and bear little resemblance to the simpler struggles outside. Briefly the situation was that the city oligarchy was divided against itself. The victualling interests—fishmongers, grocers, vintners, etc.—were exceptionally strong owing to the diversity of the London population.

In smaller towns with simpler industrial structures, the victualling interests were usually deprived of monopoly privileges in the interests of cheap food for the manufacturing elements. In London the consumers were too divided to dominate an interest serving so large a market. Furthermore, leading victuallers strengthened their hand by dabbling in other forms of enterprise such as the wool export. The victuallers were interested in maintaining a monopoly in the London food market. Consequently they were hostile to the free access of foreign traders. They also actively disliked the power of the King's Marshal in Southwark, which was used to bring in fish to break the victuallers' monopoly.

On the other hand the drapers, leading the smaller manufacturing crafts, stood for free trade (and therefore free prices) in victuals. They wished to break the victuallers' monopoly, as it had been broken, or never allowed to develop, in other towns. In leading the consumers' interests, the drapers' party found itself allied to the chief party of the nobility, that of John of Gaunt. The territorial magnates had always tended to favour free trade in the interests of cheap imported victuals. Gaunt himself was also interested in organising an expedition to Spain. His plans were being obstructed by those interested in wool export, many of whom were London victuallers. The latter wanted to attack France by way of Flanders, and set up a wool staple controlled by themselves in the Low Countries.

The drapers had considerable popular support for their cheap food policy, and also for a policy of broadening the elections to the London Common Council, to be based on craft rather than ward representation. But there were other aspects to their policy which were not popular. Many journeymen and small master craftsmen hated the drapers, whom they rightly regarded as their exploiters. Furthermore, the drapers had introduced Flemish weavers to undercut the English. Hence the weavers were hostile to foreigners, and therefore fell in with the anti-foreign cries of the victuallers. Moreover, Gaunt was universally hated, and the King's Marshal was regarded as an agent of the Gaunt-dominated government. So although the richer craftsmen supported the drapers' champion, John of Northampton, the impoverished weavers and other poor artisans sided with the victuallers. Although the victuallers were nominally in control of the city government in 1381, they were losing their grip under pressure from the manufacturing interest within, and the national government staffed by henchmen of Gaunt without. It is interesting to note that the aldermen who let in the Kent and Essex rebels were fishmongers—and were not punished after the suppression of the revolt.

Whilst this complicated internal struggle was developing in London the government too was being engulfed in international complications leading to war which only intensified the contradictions and difficulties already existing in England. War is often a desperate way out of difficulties. The history of the Hundred Years' War (traditionally dated 1337-1453) illustrates both these statements.

One of the most remarkable features of the reign of Edward III (1327-1377) was the relative absence of political conflict within the ranks of the ruling class during the greater part of the reign, although the taxation for the war which occupied the greater part of his reign was carried out with more than usual medieval extortion, inefficiency and corruption. The surprising fact is that the nobility wholeheartedly supported the war. This was something new in English history. Henry III's barons had, as one of their principal grievances against him, the expensive expeditions to Gascony and Poitou. Edward I managed to win the support of the barons of the Welsh marches in his wars against the Welsh because his interests coincided with theirs; and most of the leading English nobles had interests in the Welsh marches.

But he utterly failed to carry them with him in his wars against Scotland and France. The question hardly arose in Edward II's reign but there was certainly no bellicose anti-French feeling. In so far as there was any antagonism felt towards foreigners by the opposition barons during that period, it was directed against the Italian bankers with whose aid the king was attempting to make himself financially independent of the nobility. Yet Edward III's war, which began without conspicuous success and during which the most startling successes were won without design (and not followed up), was popular and roused all the romantic fighting spirit of what was in fact a bankrupt ruling class.

They supported it precisely because they were bankrupt. While it would be untrue to say that Edward and the English nobility consciously *started* the war with France because feudal exploitation at home was no longer profitable, it is no exaggeration to say that they carried on the war because they realised, as individuals, what great benefits, in the shape of loot and ransom money, were to be reaped from any of the many plundering expeditions which characterised the war.

The main reason for beginning the war was the struggle to dominate Gascony, that is, that part of South-Western France which includes the ports of Bordeaux and Bayonne. The English kings held Gascony as a fief from the French crown, and wanted to hold it as a piece of absolute property without interference from the French. The French kings had for two centuries been pursuing a policy of bringing all France under their close political control. Though they would be content to have the English king as Duke of Gascony, they wanted him as a subject, obedient to their over-riding control. Gascony was worth fighting for. It was Europe's chief wine-growing region. It produced, in addition, salt, steel, ships and other useful commodities. It had furthermore developed during two centuries of English connection a considerable degree of economic reciprocity. Gascony imported wheat and cloth from England rather than from France and the nobility of both countries had come to possess vested interests in the trade between the two countries. For the king it was a source of feudal profit, income from customs duties, and above all, of political power.

Two other factors which are usually considered to be among the causes of the Anglo-French conflict were the claim to the French throne put forward by Edward III, and the interests of the English wool-growers in the Flemish market. Both were in fact secondary considerations in the war. The claim to the French throne was based on formally valid genealogical arguments, but Edward III did not take it seriously as a war aim. Its main use was to salve the conscience of those who, like certain sections of the Flemish bourgeoisie or the Duke of Brittany, had other good reasons for renouncing their allegiance to the King of France. Its value for Edward III can be judged from the terms of the Treaty of Brétigny (1360) in which he willingly abandoned the claim to the French throne for absolute sovereignty over an enlarged Duchy of Gascony.

The almost complete monopoly by England over the supply of raw wool for the cloth industries of Flanders was also used by Edward III and his government as an instrument to further their main war aims. The county of Flanders, containing the great and powerful cloth towns of Bruges, Ghent and Ypres, and a host of smaller ones, was a fief of the king of France. The Count of Flanders was a faithful vassal of the French crown. He was also hated by the majority of the Flemish burgesses. By threatening to stop their supply of wool, the English obliged the cloth interests to expel the Count and take over Flanders, and to assume at first an attitude of neutrality, then of open alliance with England. The control of the wool supply was exercised by Edward III through a staple, which was a single port or town through which all exported wool had to pass. The establishment of the staple in a Flemish town was naturally a great advantage for the Flemings. It was also an advantage to the small circle of unscrupulous English war contractors and financiers who controlled the staple on the king's (and their own) behalf. It was not liked by the English growers, who preferred the free access of foreign buyers to the growing districts, through whose competition the price of wool would be put up. Neither was the foreign staple liked by those English merchants and cloth manufacturers who were excluded from the small circle of monopolists who controlled it. The staple question roused a whole number of sharp political controversies during the war period, but one thing is certain: no class in English society supported the war with France in order to obtain a preferential market for English wool. France was not a competitor, and the English monopoly was sufficiently complete for any buyers in Flanders or any other part of France to take the wool on English terms, not on their own.

It has already been stated that one of the important features of the war was that it was a common rallying ground for the whole English nobility. There were, of course, political battles during the war, mostly arising from the question of finance and the conduct of the war. The crisis of 1340 was brought about by such questions. But it was in no way a fundamental crisis. It was not comparable with the struggles of Henry III's reign between 1259 and 1265, or with events of the previous reign, which culminated in the assassination of the king by his wife and her lover in 1327. These bitter political struggles of the earlier period, like those later during Richard II's reign, or the fifteenth century Wars of the Roses, were real struggles for state power. Although at times these political struggles had the appearance of an attempt by the great nobles to limit the arbitrary power of the crown, this aspect is much exaggerated by historical interpretations dating from the period of the bourgeois revolution of the seventeenth century. Closer analysis shows that it is historically false to suggest that in feudal society the king stood apart from his barons. Such theories are usually based on the idea of a state power standing above social classes, playing a neutral role in society. When the conflicts of the period are examined in detail it will usually be found that they arise from a division within the ranks of the nobility itself, one of the factions having the king on its side, and thus controlling the machinery of state.

For the reasons already stated, then, the nobility during the greater part of the reign of Edward III was very little divided against itself. However, during the war period, a number of developments occurred which made the later conflicts all the fiercer when they did take place. These developments were partly the direct consequence of the war mobilisation, partly the result of inevitable tendencies in feudal society; the most important of them was the diminution of the great nobility as a class. The wealth of society—in this age, of course, mainly the amount of land owned—became concentrated in ever fewer hands. By the end of Edward III's reign the greater number of the old earldoms and baronies were in the hands of a narrow group of less than ten great magnates, most of them members of the royal family or closely related by blood or marriage. This was the result of a process which had begun under Edward I. An important result of the close family ties between the crown and the great nobility was that dynastic claims to the throne added justification to the claims of each faction to control of the state machine. The fierce internecine wars amongst the nobility at the end of the fourteenth century and during the fifteenth century were in a literal sense family quarrels, and all dated back to this period of comparative peace amongst the ruling group.

In addition to this concentration of the landed power in the narrowing circle of nobles, the military forces at their disposal became easier to mobilise and more efficient than in earlier days. By the period of the Hundred Years' War the old system by which knights provided military service in return for a grant in perpetuity of landed property (the knight's fee) was abandoned. The eleventh and twelfth century assessments of knight service had been reduced by Edward I, and he was only able to mobilise a host of about 230 knights and 300 men-at-arms from the whole of England. In order, therefore, to get a sufficiently numerous, and above all sufficiently well disciplined army for his Welsh wars, Edward I based recruitment not on service for land held, but on service for pay. He contracted with his earls and barons that they should produce in the field a given number of well-equipped knights and men-at-arms to be paid on the basis of 2s. per day for the ordinary knight. So that although the social composition of the army remained as before, a reflection of the hierarchy of the landowning nobility, the development of commodity production had made it possible to organise it on a much more flexible basis.

By the period of the French wars, this military system was fully established. The crown made contracts with the leading members of the nobility for troops of soldiers, usually for the duration of the campaign, for six months or a year. But the nobility began in its turn to make sub-contracts. In order always to have available a force big enough to get booty on the looting expeditions in France, each noble built up a strong permanent retinue of knights and men-at-arms, engaged for life by indenture. The noble promised a certain rate of pay, the replacement of horses lost in battle, a share in booty and in the ransoms of captured enemies. The knight promised to serve his lord's interests in peace and war. Thus, to take an example from the period of the rising, the leader of the most organised of the noble factions, John of Gaunt, Duke of Lancaster and heir to the earldoms of Leicester, Derby and Lincoln, had a permanent retinue of 227 knights and squires—merely a nucleus, of course, of the much larger force he could employ on special occasions. These armed retinues usually wore the uniform or "livery" of their employer, a habit which could of course only exacerbate existing divisions amongst the nobility; they terrorised the countryside, especially where the influence of their lord was strong. No man could expect justice from local officials of the crown or in the local or county courts if his opponent was backed or "maintained" by the great man and his retinue. Consequently most men tried to buy themselves into the great lord's retinue—or at any rate into his favour, into his "good lordship" as they put it. The burden of this terrorism and the expense of these private armies was of course ultimately borne by the peasantry.

It was after 1360 when the French began to recover, when the war began to go against the English, and to fizzle out in a series of disastrous and unprofitable expeditions such as that of Gaunt in 1373, that political quarrels among the ruling class reappeared. Robbed of their prey in France, the nobles began to rend each other. In 1376, the year of the first big political crisis since 1340, the Lancastrian party of John of Gaunt was the obvious target, since Gaunt was virtually in control of the state. Edward III was in his dotage and the Black Prince on his death-bed. The main grounds for the opposition's attack were the failure of the war in France and the utter corruption of the government. The current war profiteers were Lord Latimer and two London merchants, Lyons and Peche, all creatures of Gaunt. Their financial juggling, however, was nothing new. Such activities had been inseparable from the financing of the war, from the very first years when the wool staple and the customs had been put in the hands of a small group every bit as corrupt as Lyons and Latimer.

But in 1376 began a real battle for power amongst the magnate factions. This battle continued with occasional truces, with considerable interchanges of personnel, of immediate objectives, of slogans and of methods, for over a century. For the Parliament of 1376 achieved no more than an illusory victory over the strongly entrenched Lancastrians. It merely exposed the rottenness of the disintegrating feudal state. It certainly did *not,* as has often been claimed, mark a victory for the House of Commons as the representative institution of the gentry and the bourgeoisie. The Speaker of the House of Commons, Peter de la Mare, made brave speeches against Gaunt and government corruptions, but he was not representing a new class in society. He was the steward of the Earl of March, the leader of the baronial faction opposing Gaunt. At this period, the lesser nobility were but pawns in the hands of the great lords, and their class interests in all important matters coincided. It was the lesser nobility in the Commons who had pressed for the fullest implementation of Government measures under the Statutes of Labourers. It was the borough and county Members of Parliament who were among the special targets of the revolutionary peasants and artisans in 1381.

Although political re-shuffles on the death of Edward III and the accession of Richard II in 1377 glossed over for a time the antagonisms revealed in 1376, the ruling class was by no means a united body. The intrigue of rival factions for control of the state could not be resolved either by temporary compromise or by desertions from one party to another. The glaring contradictions between war aims and available resources, always present in medieval states, could be no longer forgotten, as before, in greed for the rich loot of France. The Parliaments which pressed for efficient and successful wars were now beginning to jib at paying the bill. The speed with which Edward III had spent the fabulous ransoms negotiated at Brétigny (including three million crowns for the captured French king) showed the landlords and the burgesses—the main contributors to taxation—that their money was disappearing down a bottomless drain. On the other hand, their illusions about the possibility of profit from war were still strong, for whilst it went well it *had* been terribly profitable for all the important leading figures amongst the nobility and the merchant oligarchs of the City of London. Their solution was to shift the burden of taxation directly on to the poorer sections of the urban and rural populations. A poll tax was voted in the Northampton Parliament of 1380, modelled on one levied three years previously, but now three times as heavy. In an attempt to make it appear a progressive tax it provided for the relief of poor taxpayers by increased payments from their rich neighbours. There was a mass evasion of the tax collectors, and the government's attempt to collect a second time from those who had escaped the first was the immediate cause of the revolt.

It was, however, nothing more than an immediate cause. All conditions for an uprising were ripe. All the *ruled* sections of society for various reasons were no longer prepared to submit to the old ways of rule. The *rulers* were divided amongst themselves, bankrupt, and incapable of carrying out even their own most cherished projects. Little is known of the organisation or the ideological preparation for a revolt, but it existed in some degree. It is true that by the very nature of its occupation and composition the peasantry was incapable of coherent and farseeing political organisation. Talk of the Great Society which was supposed to have organised the revolt on a national scale can largely be traced to ruling class suspicions, recorded in the monastic chronicles and the indictments of rebels after the suppression of the revolt. This does not mean that there was not a good degree of common understanding between village and village, and between region and region (as for instance between Kent and Essex, between South Lincolnshire and Norfolk). But this understanding probably went no further than the knowledge each had of the other's woe, a knowledge that was not only spread by direct contact of peasants in local markets, but by pedlars and preachers.

It was preachers especially who must have given shape to ideas developing spontaneously in peasant minds. At this point, therefore, we must consider what were the ideas of the opinion-formers of feudal society, both high and low; how did they come by these ideas; and how did they express and transmit them to the classes on whose behalf they spoke and wrote.

CHAPTER THREE

# THE IDEALS OF FEUDAL SOCIETY: I.

## *Opinion-Formers*

THE PREVAILING ideas of fourteenth century society were those of society's rulers. But since, as we have seen, their society was in the process of dissolution, it is only natural that there were reflections of this dissolution in the realm of ideas. Official society was divided within itself. It was no longer the poor and oppressed or the artisans and merchants alone who were the fountainhead of heresy, but what should have been the centre of orthodoxy, the University of Oxford.

Those who formulated the ideas of the official society of this period fall into three general categories: the lawyers, the clergy and the litterateurs. The lawyers were in most cases laymen and were responsible for some of the most coherent statements of medieval political and social theory. They were intimately concerned with the political problems of feudal society because it was they who presided over, or pleaded before, the courts—both private and public—through which medieval government was carried out. They were closely associated in everyday life with the great lords, lay and ecclesiastical, with the king and with the members of the royal administration. They were expert in the land law which was so important in a society still mainly agricultural. They were also considered to be the repositories of the law and custom which governed the relations of the king and his barons and were therefore involved in the many political disputes which divided the ruling class in the thirteenth and fourteenth centuries. They were also the creators of the network of law which kept the peasant bound down to the soil, to the will of his lord. Although conflicts of loyalty might have affected them as between king and barons, or different parties amongst the baronage, they were unanimous in their attitude towards the peasantry, and adequately expressed the outlook of their masters, all of whom, whatever their temporary disagreements, lived on the product of the peasants' toil.

It was the clergy, both regular and secular (that is those who belonged to the various orders of monks and friars and those who did not), who were concerned with more abstract theory. Lawyers were trained to deal with practical problems. Those members of the clergy who went to the university were first of all given a basic education in Latin grammar and in logic. This led on to an Arts course based (from the thirteenth century) on the contemporary interpretations of the works of Aristotle. They also might go on to specialise in canon (that is church) law or theology. The most characteristic and important forms of speculation at the universities were philosophy and theology, and what the clerical students (for there were no laymen at the Universities) learnt there, they carried out into the world after finishing their studies.

The successful Master of Arts from the Universities of Oxford or Cambridge had open to him a number of careers, though all were crowded. Promotion in church or state, or both, were possible. The royal administration was principally manned by clerics, most of whom remained in the lowest orders of the hierarchy of the church and never became priests. The state machine was expanding greatly in the fourteenth century. First there were the great state offices such as the Chancery and the Exchequer; then there were the smaller offices of the King's Household, such as the Wardrobe and the

Chamber, whose functions extended far beyond the administration of the King's personal affairs. These offices provided many jobs for the clergy, from the humblest writer up to the powerful confidential clerks who were sometimes accused, by indignant barons from the provinces, of formulating royal policy. Although most of the leading pleaders and judges were laymen, clerics also found employment in the courts of King's Bench and Common Pleas, and with the itinerant and local judicial commissions which were such an important feature of the administration at this period. The complicated diplomatic negotiations which were an essential part of fourteenth century wars, truces and peace-making, were also occasions for the employment of many an aspiring cleric.

Clerics were employed not only by the central organs of the state but also locally. As a counterpart to the growth of the offices of state in London, local administration became more involved. Hence in every county town every sheriff had to have a staff of clerks, as did other officials such as coroners, escheators, bailiffs and the like. Much local government was still in private hands, so many clerics found employment in all grades of private administration. The big estates, as has already been mentioned, had an elaborate hierarchy of officials from stewards and receivers down to manorial reeves and bailiffs. Many of the actual administrative officials themselves were clerics, such as the Receiver-General and subordinate receivers in the estates of the Duke of Lancaster. But apart from these, all records and accounts had to be kept by clerics. On the estates of Merton College, Oxford, every manor reeve had his own personal clerk. Then in addition to private estates, many local government areas and courts, whose business was the same as that carried on in other places by royal officials, came under the control of private individuals—barons, abbots and bishops. These were known as "liberties" or "franchises" and some (such as the Soke of Peterborough) have left their mark on the map today. These franchise courts were largely administered by clerics.

The Church was almost as elaborate in its administration as the central government and therefore absorbed many clerics in its routine as distinct from its purely religious activities. The temporal possessions of the church, that is the landed and other property which it held in the same way as lay proprietors, were enormous in extent, consisting of the estates, large and small, of bishops, deans and chapters, collegiate churches, abbeys, priories and the like. The other possessions of the church, which accrued to it because of its religious functions, such as glebe land, tithes, altar offerings, also formed a significant proportion of the sources of church income and had to be collected, accounted for, and otherwise administered. Then the church as the supreme organ of spiritual and moral discipline, as dispenser of the sacraments necessary to salvation, was an organisation with an intricate machinery absorbing many clerical workers. The ecclesiastical courts, which dealt with cases involving morals, matrimony and oaths (including wills), were as elaborate in their organisation as the lay courts. Every diocese had its administration with a hierarchy of officials from the bishop downwards, through archdeacon and rural dean to the parish clergy, all of which involved the work of clerics other than those who were directly concerned with religious duties. In fact, of the whole clerical order in fourteenth century England, comparatively few must have been engaged on the task which to the ordinary man seemed to be the main justification for their existence—the saving of souls.

From this brief description of clerical employment it will be seen that the clergy could not be considered a socially homogeneous group, were we to look no further than the contrast between the lordly bishops and the humble clerk writing up the manorial account. But another factor sharpened the contrast between the practice and the pretensions of the church, and in so doing intensified the political conflicts in fourteenth-century society.

It was the habit of kings, princes, bishops and barons to reward faithful clerical servants by granting them church benefices, usually the office of rector of a parish. They were able to dispose of parish churches and their revenues in this way because most parish churches had originally been founded and endowed by lords of manors, so that the right to present the priest to the living remained a private right. Since, owing to the imperfect development of the taxation system, the funds for the payment of civil servants were inadequate, and since it was worth while keeping the services of an efficient clerk by giving him promotion as good as he could get elsewhere, this handing over of benefices to men for other reasons than their suitability as parish priests dominated the distribution of religious offices. Nor did it stop at the parish level, but largely determined the distribution of preferments at all levels up to and including the rank of archbishop. For several centuries, in fact, promotion to the majority of bishoprics had been for political services.

A complicating factor since the middle of the thirteenth century was that a fresh set of competitors for profitable benefices in the English church made their appearance. The Papal administration was even more intricate and even less able to reward its servants than that of kings and national churches. The Popes had found a partial solution in "providing" those whom they wished to reward—often English clerics, but also in many cases foreigners—to benefices in England and elsewhere. This the Pope claimed to be able to do by virtue of his plenitude of power as head of the church. Papal provisions of this sort not only annoyed those of the native clergy who were deprived of advantages they considered to be their right, but also threatened the rights of those lords (mainly ecclesiastical), who had the presentation to benefices. This is an important factor in such anti-Papal feeling as existed at the time.

Italian priests employed at the Papal curia did not of course take up their parish duties in the benefices to which they were provided. Nor as a general rule did the English clergy who were presented to benefices as a reward for services rendered or expected. In fact it would have been impossible for them to do so, even had their other duties permitted them. For most of them enjoyed not one but several benefices at the same time. These men were known as "pluralists". A good example is a priest who was a Bachelor of Law in the service of the Bishop of Hereford and who was promoted by successive bishops, until by 1356 he was enjoying the revenues of six benefices. Sometimes the duties attached to the benefice were utterly neglected, but in the case of the care of souls in a parish the absentee foreigner or pluralist would appoint a poor priest to do his job for a wage. The parish revenues from the glebe land, tithes, and so on, went to the absentee.

Some priests were put to work in parishes as wage-earners for another reason. Many churches had been "appropriated" by monasteries, that is the monasteries had been given so many rights in various parishes—the right to present the priest, rights over tithes—that eventually the monastery became in law the corporate rector, as it were, of the parish with full rights to the parish revenues. Since a corporate body could not do the duties of a priest, a poor priest was employed as a vicar with a small fraction of the tithes or at a very small wage, to carry out the duty of saving the souls of the parishioners.

It cannot be said that all members of the clergy were in possession of the learning of which the church was the principal dispenser. Only a minority of clerks went to the university. The majority of the parish clergy, and certainly of the clerks in what we would consider purely secular employment, were extremely ignorant. Nevertheless, because the clergy were almost the only literate members of society, the theories of ecclesiastical speculators in the schools and universities had the chance of percolating down, probably in greatly altered form, to the lowest ranks of the clergy.

The fourteenth century was a great age of sermon manuals, both in Latin and English, which enabled parish preachers to learn and to retail to their flocks not only the purely religious ideas, but also more general views about the structure of society and the rights and duties of the classes which composed it. But as will be seen later, orthodox theories about political rights and duties could be double edged. What would be the actual effect of a sermon that dealt with political and social matters depended to a considerable extent both on the preacher and on his audience. Obviously an archbishop or a bishop preaching about social obligations to the lords, knights and burgesses of Parliament, would approach the matter from a different angle from that of a poor stipendiary priest preaching to an audience of peasants whose poverty and lack of social rights were much the same as his own. The church in fact was divided into classes with as incompatible interests as those of lay society. The rebel peasantry therefore owed a great debt to such members of the lower clergy as John Ball, and no doubt to others less famous. Christian belief then, as on many occasions since its foundation, could be a revolutionary creed in the hands of the common people.

Although the clergy were much the most important section of opinion-formers in fourteenth-century England among all classes of society, we must not forget the poets and other *littérateurs* who in their verses and stories expressed the outlook on life of the feudal ruling class and of the upper ranks of the burgesses. These poets were not normally members of the top rank of the ruling class, although in twelfth-century Europe robber-barons such as Bertrand de Born and the war-like and predatory Richard I had turned their hand to courtly lyrics in French or Provençal. The poets whose works both expressed and influenced the outlook of the ruling elements of medieval English society were, whether laymen or clerics, for the most part members of the lesser nobility or dependent entirely on noble patrons. Geoffrey Chaucer, client of John of Gaunt, is an example. Most of his predecessors in the field of romance are of unknown name and origin, but their rhymed romances betray the social environment of their authors. Whether their themes are derived from French epics about Charlemagne, or French allegories, or Celtic legends about Arthur and his knights, or from tales of Anglo-Saxon times, they are all reduced to a common pattern as far as the reflection of social life is concerned. The heroes and knights, barons and kings and their exploits in love, in battle or in religion faithfully represent the feudal outlook of loyalty, caste, and unquestioning devotion to established religion. Within these narrow limits, from which (till Chaucer) all classes outside the sacred confines of the ennobled were excluded, there was full scope for allegory, description, and psychological analysis. Perhaps the extreme symbolism and the recurring theme of dreams and visions was the consequence of the narrow social exclusiveness of much of this literature, and its consequent abstraction from reality. At any rate it is clear that a nobility brought up on literature of which Malory's *Morte d'Arthur* is a late but characteristic example would receive a rude shock when it heard the sound described by Professor Eileen Power as "the clatter of the Bundschuh[1] on the road to freedom".

Of course the English and Anglo-French writers of the

[1] The peasant's shoe, symbol of peasant revolt in Germany in the early sixteenth century. cf. F. Engels, *Peasant War in Germany*.

thirteenth and fourteenth centuries did not consist only of those retelling the stories of Arthur and Charlemagne. But they are put first here because this artificial code of chivalry which they popularised was so prominent in the life of the English nobility in the years preceding the rising. There were also the historians. Froissart, the clerical knight from Northern France, author of *The Chronicles of England, France and Spain,* writes entirely from the standpoint of those for whom the chivalric romances were intended. There were others whose viewpoint, while still that of the nobility, was different. Amongst these are the monastic chroniclers, whose writings are of immense value for our knowledge of English history. Although the monastic ideal prescribed isolation from the world, the monastic chroniclers reflected the shrewd political judgments of the abbots and priors of England, who were barons before they were men of religion. Many monasteries were frequently visited by the king and the lay nobility, so that monastic historians in the great houses near London had many opportunities to get information of what was going on in the world. The thirteenth and fourteenth century chronicles of the Abbey of St. Albans often rise above their chronicle form to the dignity of real historical writing, complete with the class bias which is not, of course, confined to the medieval monks. These historical writings are important both as indications of opinion and as formers both of contemporary and later opinion. The indebtedness of chroniclers to each other shows that their writings must have been widely disseminated. And the very history of the rising itself shows their importance. For from the historians of the sixteenth century to the "scientific" historians of the twentieth century, the violent class prejudice of the chroniclers, such as that of the all but expropriated Abbey of St. Albans, have coloured assessments of the events and the aims of the revolt ever since.

*Official Opinions*

It has been shown that by the fourteenth century one of the most characteristic features of feudal society in its hey-day had disappeared. This was the arrangement by which all members of the feudal nobility below the king held their land in return for the rendering of knight-service. But although medieval armies were no longer organised on the basis of knight service much of the outlook which was involved in the relation between lord and military vassal still dominated the social and political conceptions of all sections of the ruling class. In the eleventh and twelfth centuries, the vassal on receipt of the land for which he rendered military service to the lord performed the act of homage and swore allegiance. This created what was then considered to be a solemn and binding relationship, and the strength of the tie was all the greater since the rendering of homage by man to lord had its ancestry in the last days of tribal society, when members of warrior bands swore a similar oath to their chieftain.

This relationship of lord and vassal was very important socially at the beginning of feudal society when the ruling class had not yet evolved a machinery of state and when, in addition to the fundamental social conflict between lord and serf, tendencies towards division and mutual conflict amongst the nobles were very strong. The relationship was considerably strengthened by the growth of strong emotional and ethical associations. The vassal's duty to his lord became not merely the performance of his contractual obligations, but a matter of life and death, for the true vassal's regard for his lord was held to be the most important of all obligations, charged with a much greater emotional content than, for instance, the relationship between man and wife. Fidelity was upheld as the most noble of virtues, and the most heinous of villainies was treason to a lord. The Anglo-Saxon laws of the ninth and tenth centuries state that such treason cannot be compensated, though minor matters such as homicide could. One of the greatest of the feudal epics, the *Chanson de Roland,* which was written down in the early part of the twelfth century, tells of an incident resulting from treachery during Charlemagne's wars against the Arabs of Spain towards the end of the eighth century. The feudal attitude towards treason is illustrated at the end of the poem when Ganelon, the arch-traitor, is punished by being torn into pieces by four horses, each attached to one of his limbs by a rope, and driven in opposite directions.

Self-interest, and conflicting loyalties when vassals held from more than one lord, produced many breaches of the feudal contract in practice, but these did not destroy the hold of its principles over men's minds, nor were these principles without importance as an element of social cohesion. They laid the basis for an outlook on society as a whole which affected political ideas expressed by those not directly concerned with the feudal contract. The subordination of the lower ranks of society to the higher, the denial of social equality, of natural political rights, the conception of a fixed and unchangeable hierarchy, are all implicit in relations existing between greater and lesser members of the ruling class. It can therefore be imagined how much more strongly these ideas were applied to the relations between the nobility as a whole and the serfs.

Yet there were in fact elements in the ideas built around the relations of lord and vassal which contradicted strict conceptions of hierarchy and subordination. The feudal relationship was a contract by which the lord gave the vassal not only land, but protection. Some feudal theorists even went as far as to say that the mutual obligations of lord and vassal were of the same weight, except for the reverence which the vassal owed to the lord. Hence vassals sometimes might have the right, even the duty, of renouncing their allegiance to the lord if he on his side broke the feudal contract. In fact lords often did break the contract, usually by the exploitation of the financial side of their vassals' obligations to them beyond what were considered to be reasonable limits. The Norman kings of England of the eleventh and twelfth centuries on more than one occasion roused the opposition of their vassals because they tried to solve their financial problems by (to give only one example) charging the heirs of their vassals exorbitant sums for the right to succeed to the fiefs, instead of the sums fixed by custom. Similar over-straining of the primitive machinery of feudal obligations led to the political crisis of 1215 when King John signed the baronial Magna Carta.

Now it would clearly be extremely dangerous to the ruling class as a whole if the peasantry began to adopt the same sort of attitude to their lords as the lesser elements in the hierarchy of the feudal nobility did on occasion to the higher. Ideas often spill over the bounds which are meant to contain them, and peasant communities all had immemorial customs dating from freer days which could be used against attempts by lords to intensify exploitation. It was therefore an important function of the legal theoriests of the twelfth and thirteenth centuries to confirm in theory what was so evident in practice—that the relationships between the higher and lower ranks of the feudal aristocracy had nothing to do with the relationships between the aristocracy as a whole and the peasantry as a whole. They did this by borrowing considerably from the Roman laws of slavery and from other laws of the late Roman Empire which bound the peasant to the soil whether he was legally of servile status or not.

It was laid down clearly that the serf was a human being who had no rights against his lord save that his lord could not kill him (this in itself was an advance on ancient slavery).

The livelihood and property of the serf was dependent entirely on the will of the lord. Naturally the land which the serf worked as "his" holding was considered to be the lord's property, but in addition any chattels or money which the serf accumulated were the lord's possession. This led to the doctrine that the serf could not purchase his freedom from the lord because in so doing he would be offering the lord money which was already his. A third person always had to purchase the charter of manumission which would make the serfs free. Serfs could not buy and sell land among themselves, for transfers could only take place by surrender of the land in the lord's court. It was up to the lord or his representative to determine the terms on which it was re-granted. Any conception of the peasant having rights against the lord following the terms of a contract similar to that prevailing amongst the nobles had, therefore, no place in feudal theory. The only factor which restrained the exploitation of serfs by lord was the strength and cohesion of the peasant community, expressed in its village customs, and the need of the lord, in an age of sparse population, to maintain a sufficient labour force on the land to produce the surplus on which he lived.

The needs of the situation, and the use of the laws of slavery both of the Roman Empire and of the Teutonic barbarian tribes, tended towards the reduction of all the peasants to a servile caste, rather than simply an exploited class. Theories of servile blood were elaborated, so that (as already mentioned) cases of dispute about villein status in the courts involved the working out of lengthy genealogical trees. The lawyers and chroniclers of the ruling class began to speak of the contamination of free blood resulting from intermarriage between free and serf. Since at the same time certain types of agricultural service and certain forms of customary payment were being taken as indices of the servile condition of tenants holding the lands on which these services and payments were assessed, the conception of a servile caste embraced more and more of the peasantry. It is true that there were movements in the opposite direction. Even some of the lawyers who were in some ways defining serfdom to the disadvantage of those of hitherto undefined condition were at the same time (like the Englishman Bracton in the thirteenth century) suggesting some safeguards for free men who happened to take villein land to cultivate. But such tendencies were exceptional in thirteenth-century England. Even the (always theoretical) Christian conception of the equality of all men on earth, since all were equal in the eyes of God, was breaking down. Aristotle's justification of slavery as a natural institution was taken over by such theoreticians as Thomas Aquinas together with other teachings of Aristotle which were being made known for the first time in the medieval world. A monkish lampoon written in 1276 in England could end with the slogan, "What could a serf do but serve? A pure serf he shall be, lacking liberty, and his son after him."

Such an outlook on the majority of the medieval population naturally affected the conception of society as a whole. The division of society into classes was frankly recognised, and these classes were seen as admitting of no penetrations from the lower ranks. But since this hierarchical outlook on society was formulated by the ruling class it was naturally not seen as based on exploitation. The different classes in society were each assigned a function, and for their comfort, the peasants were assured that without them society could not exist. All the more reason therefore that they should remain in the station to which God had called them.

The hierarchy was variously depicted. The fundamental division was not so much between the free and the unfree (important though this may have been in the law courts) as between the noble and the non-noble. It is interesting to note that this cleavage was stressed especially at a time when facts were making the idea nonsensical—at the end of the middle ages when socially and economically certain sections of the bourgeoisie were much nearer to the nobility than they were to the peasants. Some of them were pressing on the heels of the nobility and this it was that made the nobles highly conscious of the peculiar colour of their blood. French authors in the fifteenth century referred to the rich and powerful burgesses of the Flemish towns as "villeins", as indeed does the chronicler of the Abbey of St. Albans when referring to the rebellious townsmen of St. Albans, who were certainly free men in the eyes of the law.

Another extremely common medieval division of society was between lay nobles, churchmen, and peasants, that is, those who fight, those who pray, and those who work. Here it should be noticed that the fighting done by the nobles was in theory for the protection of all who prayed and worked, the prayers were for the protection of all, and the work for the sustenance of all. It is noteworthy, too, that the burgesses are omitted from this categorisation. Sometimes this functional view of the hierarchy was expressed allegorically. The most familiar analogy of the body politic was the human body and the different classes in society were compared to appropriate limbs and members. The head was the prince, the hands were the nobility, the soul was religion, and the feet the peasants. There were other variations, but the directing organs of the body were always compared to the members of the ruling class.

Man's tendency to create God in his own image and then to assume that the reverse was the case has its reflection in medieval views of society. The social hierarchy was thought of as the earthly reflection of the heavenly order. God in heaven was flanked by archangels and supported by an ascending scale of saints, cherubs, angels and other celestial beings. This arrangement in fact of course reflected the earthly hierarchies, but served as the justification of the status quo. For if the earthly hierarchy were a reflection of the heavenly hierarchy, any attempt to alter the relationship of the parts in this divinely articulated arrangement would be sinful. Society looked at in this way was just lacking in any element permitting change as society considered as analogous to the human body. Nor should it be thought that medieval thinkers considered that the earthly hierarchy resembled the heavenly hierarchy only because such a form of social organisation was the best both for human beings and for the saints and angels. The social structure on earth was literally envisaged as mirroring the heavenly order. An all-embracing unity in the universe under God determined the grading of all creation from the humblest member of human society up to Him sitting in Heaven. The pattern was the same at all stages.

CHAPTER FOUR

# THE IDEAS OF FEUDAL SOCIETY: II

## *Divisions of Official Opinions*

REAL CRACKS in this cosmic unity made hierarchical theories of society difficult to maintain, and of these the political conflict between the church and the various states, national monarchies, was the most important. From the middle of the eleventh century European feudalism was recovering political and economic stability. The nobility was consolidating its wealth and political power. But there existed in every European country a contradictory situation within the ranks of the nobility. Churchmen—bishops and abbots—were members of the nobility with the same basic economic and social interests as the barons. But the lay nobility, from the kings downwards, were attempting to bring church property under their control in their own countries. The churchmen naturally objected, though many archbishops and bishops, as the principal advisers of the kings, were perplexed by divided political loyalties. The Papacy attempted to organise the universal church as a political force, as a state, separate from the secular, geographically determined, feudal states which composed Christian Europe. The Popes negotiated on equal terms with German Emperors, and French and English kings, fought them, sometimes humiliated them. They organised fifth columns of churchmen in the state; their agents intrigued with one ruler to set him against another; crusades were organised, newly conquered territories were brought under the Pope's feudal overlordship. The

Papacy's political battle for the overlordship of Europe against the German Holy Roman Emperors in the eleventh, twelfth and thirteenth centuries filled the European political scene. But it was replaced in the fourteenth century by a conflict much more dangerous fundamentally not only to the Papal political power but to medieval political theories, Papal or otherwise.

This new conflict was between the international Papacy and the feudal states of Europe. By the fourteenth century the principal states of Western Europe, England and France, were no longer agglomerations of semi-autonomous earldoms and baronies held together by a king who was merely the first among his fellow feudal lords. The ruling classes had become concentrated; the lesser local jurisdictions were being replaced by the activities of complicated centralised bureaucracies. As yet, this developing machinery of state was not national in scale. In the fourteenth century, in France as well as in England, one or two of the most powerful nobles were attempting to imitate the machinery of royal government for their own territories. John of Gaunt's Palatine Duchy of Lancaster is an example, though not as spectacular as the French Duchy of Burgundy. But the elaboration of the royal state apparatus during this period was preparing the way for the absolutisms of the sixteenth century and afterwards, even though, for the time being, fierce rivalries among a narrow circle of nobles postponed the firm establishment of a unified state. Nevertheless the drawing together of the ruling class, the clear crystallisation of a state apparatus at its disposal, made it look with jealousy on the economic and political claims of the papacy, particularly those encroachments on the privileges of the nobility known as Papal provisions (see above, p. 55).

In the wake of the suspicion of Papal financial expedients came a renewed attitude of hostility and suspicion on the part of some elements among the nobility and the bourgeoisie towards the church in England. There were clearly discernable trends critical of the church hierarchy and its wealth, which (in spite of numerous clerics among the critics) may be termed anti-clerical. In general, anti-clericalism was not associated with any criticism of the church's fundamental teachings. Wycliffe and his followers were eventually denounced as heretics, but they were not the only anti-clericals.

The most deeply founded anti-clericalism came from the lower strata of articulate society, the merchants and the lesser nobility, and their anti-clericalism may even have been succoured by popular feeling from below, from the peasantry. This popular anti-clericalism was provoked by the clear contradiction between the ethical teachings of the church and the behaviour of its most prominent clergy. The wealth of the older monastic orders had as early as the first years of the twelfth century been observed to have produced an outlook among abbots and monks which was the reverse of the poverty, chastity and obedience prescribed in their vows. At the end of the twelfth century even Richard I, when asked by a preacher to get rid of his three evil daughters, Pride, Avarice and Luxury, offered to give Pride to the Templars, Avarice to the Cistercians, and Luxury to the Bishops. The prestige of the religious orders had been raised somewhat at the beginning of the thirteenth century by the new orders of Friars, the Franciscans and the Dominicans. Whilst the Franciscans only held for a short time, and the Dominicans never, to the ideal of apostolic poverty, their learning and zeal lasted for longer, but their reputation was wearing very thin by the middle of the fourteenth century. Many of the political poems of the late thirteenth and early fourteenth centuries satirise the monasteries. A poem of Edward I's reign, for instance, describes the Rule and Life of the monks and nuns of the Order of Fair Ease, where all the pleasures of the flesh are to be indulged as a matter of principle. It is worth noting that all classes are welcomed into the Order except peasants:

> "For it would shame the Order if poor man or villein were to gain a position where he could have mastery, for he would be most like to the wolf which devours the sheep."

Anti-clerical satire in the fourteenth century is most pungent perhaps where it was least savage, in the poems of Geoffrey Chaucer. Chaucer came from the merchant class and was most of his life a member, in different branches, of the state bureaucracy—for instance in the customs. But as a young man he had been a squire in the household of the first wife of John of Gaunt, Duke of Lancaster, and was probably a political supporter of Gaunt during the rest of his life. Clearly he represents the outlook of the nobility, the rich merchants and the successful "civil servants". There is nothing in the least revolutionary about his writing. But no one laid bare more than he does in his Canterbury Tales the avarice, self-indulgence, and denial of all that the religious life was supposed to mean, of monks, friars, nuns and other clerics. The only members of the clerical order who come well out of his Prologue are the parish parson and the Oxford scholar. In both cases the aspect of their character for which Chaucer clearly intends us to feel most sympathy is their indifference to worldly wealth.

Chaucer provides a sort of link between the more popular form of indignation against the worldly wealth of the clergy, because of its contrast with their profession, and the hostility of upper-class laymen to clerical wealth, because they would like to get hold of it for themselves. This upper-class opposition to the clergy was sporadic and inconsistent. On two occasions during Edward III's reign clerical ministers who became the scapegoats for failures of policy, which were probably not their fault, were replaced by laymen as a consequence of a clear though temporary anti-clerical movement among the nobility. But it was always difficult for the nobility, whether of the first rank or of less importance, to keep up an anti-clerical policy. They were dependent on clerics for the efficient running of the state machine, both in its higher and lower reaches. Bishops and abbots were their friends and relations. Most lords and gentry had personal interests in religious foundations, to which they or their ancestors had contributed, and over which they had rights of hospitality and patronage. Consequently no move to confiscate monastic property went further in practice than the confiscation of the English possessions of alien (that is French) religious houses, which were taken over in 1414. The only consistent demand for the abolition of monastic and clerical wealth came from the heretical followers of Wycliffe, the Lollards, mostly members of the gentry and the forerunners of the class which was to profit most from the dissolution of the monasteries in 1536-40.

Here it is necessary to stress a very important stage in medieval social and political criticism. Criticism of the church and its institutions could not in the middle ages—or indeed as late as the seventeenth and eighteenth centuries—be anything but a criticism of society as a whole. This is obvious even if we only consider how closely inter-related were the personnel, property and jurisdiction of the church and of the lay nobility. When we also take into account the fact that official religion was mainly responsible for the ideas of official society as a whole, it becomes even more clear that a fundamental attack on feudalism could not be other than an attack on the religion of feudal society. Any attack upon the established order of society had to start as a religious heresy.

Heresy was therefore always most fiercely stamped out. Propagandists of the Empire or of the feudal monarchies often made very sharp attacks on the temporal powers of the Papacy, without departing from doctrinal orthodoxy. But, apart from the fact that in any case they were able to shelter behind their powerful employers, they were never treated with such extreme ruthlessness as were heretics who might often be preaching doctrine which on the surface seemed politically less harmful. This is no place to recount the history of medieval heresies, but a general characteristic of all those which were considered the most dangerous should be mentioned. This was the idea of the individual achievement of salvation through a direct relationship with God, the essence of the puritanism and non-conformity of the early capitalist era. Such ideas led eventually to a rejection of the sacraments of the church (such as communion, baptism, etc.) and of the hierarchy that was set up to administer the sacraments. It tended to make every man his own priest. It contradicted his dependence on established order of which the ecclesiastical was the counterpart of the secular aspect. Kings and barons were as hostile to ideas of this sort as were the clerics.

It was for ideas which were in part similar to these that the reformer John Wycliffe and his followers were condemned. It is true that Wycliffe's criticisms were formulated too late to have had any direct influence on the Peasants' Rising. Yet his movement was an important symptom of the break-up of the medieval system, not so much because he said anything new, but because of the support he got in his re-formulation of earlier criticism. Wycliffe himself was not the person who might have been expected to lead a movement of revolt of any sort. For the greater part of his life he was a prominent scholar and teacher at the University of Oxford. The sort of problems he was first concerned with were abstruse and technical philosophical problems, and the standpoint he adopted was that of extreme "realism" (that is, in so far as the term is translatable into modern terms, extreme idealism). But he found himself drawn to the consideration of more practical issues—the nature of just government, the true mission of the church, the rights of secular authority over the priesthood, the problems of church property.

Wycliffe was first officially condemned by the Pope in 1377, not yet for any attack on the fundamental Catholic doctrines, but for certain political views which were held to endanger the church's position in civil society. Not unconnected with this condemnation was the fact that Wycliffe had been employed by the government in diplomatic negotiations with the Papacy concerning the English refusal of tribute to Rome. The political views for which Wycliffe were condemned were shortly afterwards embodied in the work *On Civil Lordship*. Although they were expressed in the language of scholastic debate, and owed much to a previous writer, Richard Fitz-Ralph, Archbishop of Armagh, there were revolutionary implications contained within them. Wycliffe held that lordship exercised by persons not endowed with divine grace was no true lordship. Although Wycliffe in practice deflected the fullest revolutionary implications of this doctrine by also preaching the need to submit to even unjust rule, enough remained to make the teaching dangerous. For not only was the unjust king no true lord, but it was also implied that the spiritual head of Christendom, the Pope, might well be a man without grace, predestined to damnation. If the Pope, and the other exalted persons of the ecclesiastical hierarchy, were fallible intermediaries between man and God, the visible fabric of the organised church was dissolved.

It was this aspect of his doctrines which Wycliffe developed most strongly. Any criticism of unjust secular rulers was left abstract, and was nullified by the opposite doctrine of obedience. But the authority of the church hierarchy was further attacked by the insistence that the church must be governed according to evangelical principles. This means that the church should become, as it was in the era of its foundation, uncontaminated by secular entanglements and property. The secular state was therefore entitled to claim as its own sphere rights and property appropriated by the wealthy and powerful church. Religious orders with property as well as worldly bishops must be abolished. Such doctrines were, of course, well suited to members of the nobility and gentry who shared no part of the deep sincerity which inspired Wycliffe. These men at the best were anti-clericals who objected to clerical monopoly of government, and at the worst simply wanted to get their hands on the property of the church. It is impossible to say into which of these categories Wycliffe's patron, John of Gaunt, Duke of Lancaster, should be placed. The fact remains that even after Gaunt had ceased actively to support Wycliffe (as he had done, against the Archbishop of Canterbury, up until 1378), it was owing to his continued protection that the reformer died peacefully in 1387 in full possession of his Lutterworth parsonage. Gaunt did not approve of Wycliffe's heresy on the Eucharist and was probably affected by the attempts to accuse Wycliffe and his followers as promoters of the rising.

Wycliffe's significance, then, in connection with the rising lies not in any direct influence he or his followers had on it. It lies in the fact that he represents an important element in the break-up of medieval society. Without consciously attacking feudal order—his doctrine of lordship was feudal in inspiration—his undermining of the strongest bulwark of feudalism, the international church, was of the greatest importance. Not only in doctrine did he approach reformation ideas very closely, with his dismissal of the church hierarchy as a necessary means to salvation, but he actively promoted the achievement of salvation by individuals. He and his followers believed that it was not in the canon laws of the church that were to be found the principles of Christian conduct, but in the Bible. In having it translated into English, he put what he considered to be the key to salvation into every man's hand. The church rightly recognised that this would make her apparatus superfluous and forbade the indiscriminate placing of the Scripture into the hands of the laity. The church also reacted very strongly against the spreading of unorthodox religious and social doctrines by Wycliffite preachers. The power of the pulpit in forming public opinion and spreading official views was considerable and was recognised at this period just as it was recognised two and a half centuries later by Charles I. Consequently only certain categories of persons were allowed to preach, namely those in holy orders having the cure of souls, and others with special licences, such as university graduates, pardoners selling indulgences, friars and the like. John Ball, the rebel leader, was forbidden the use of the pulpit for his sermons, and was thereby forced to preach on village greens. Wycliffe's appreciation of the importance of direct access to the Bible for all men seeking salvation did not remain academic, and he promoted the preaching of his views by his followers, who became well known as Lollards. The success of their activity, and the fears of the ruling class not only for established religion but for established order, led to an Act of Parliament permitting punishment by burning for heresy (1401) and an Act of Convocation restricting the numbers and topics of preachers (1409).

The Lollard preachers did not become effective until after the rising, but the activities of preachers before the revolt should not be underestimated. It must be remembered that John Ball himself was said at the time of the revolt to have been preaching the social implications of primitive Christianity for twenty years. We know that his doctrine of "when Adam delved and Eve span, who was then the gentleman?" was not that of an isolated prophet. The cry for social justice was in fact almost a commonplace among preachers, including the most orthodox and respectable. John Bromyard, a Dominican friar who became Chancellor of the University of Cambridge, compiled an immense handbook for preachers some time in the second half of the fourteenth century, drawing on sermon material dating back as far as the previous century. The Dominicans (also known as the Friars Preachers) were pillars of orthodoxy, but Bromyard's work is full of the most outspoken social criticism, a social criticism to be found also in other vernacular sermons and satirical verse of the same period.

"The poor for their good works are not rewarded," says Bromyard, "but are so oppressed by the rich and powerful that however true a cause a poor man may have against a rich man in this world, it will nonetheless happen to him as it did to the lamb at the hands of the wolf . . . the poor man, indeed, if he steal the rich man's food is hung. The rich man is not punished at all for seizing the goods of the poor, even when he is worthy of the gallows." He even goes so far as to suggest for the rich and powerful: "It would be far better, therefore, for their soul that they should be drawn by horses to the gallows of the world, than that they should ride thus to the gallows of Hell." The officials of the feudal lords are described as grinding the poor "like infernal millstones, one lying stationary in peace, while the other travels round".

Preachers' vituperations against the idle rich would fill volumes. And yet many of these men who spoke so harshly, not only against the lay nobility but against the prelates of the church, remained in favour, attained high official positions, as did Bromyard, or another preacher, Brunton, who became bishop of Rochester. Two questions suggest themselves. Firstly, why do these representatives of official thought appear to have been attacking a social order of which they were the beneficiaries? Secondly, why were they allowed to make these attacks, not only without interference, but without their views hindering (in some cases at any rate) the normal processes of promotion?

The answer to the first question is that in fact they were not attacking a social order. They were defending a social order that was disintegrating. Perhaps more accurately it could be said that they were defending an ideal picture of a social order which was more than ever ceasing to correspond to reality. The fact is that these attacks on the cruelty, extravagance, ostentation and lechery of the lords were usually paralleled by attacks on what were considered to be the characteristic vices of the other classes in society, such as the avarice of the merchants, or the idleness and insubordination of the peasantry. The Christian preachers had a conception of a "balanced" society, a class hierarchy such as has already been described. In such a society each class had a different and complementary function. The king and his nobles governed and protected the weak and poor against oppression; the clergy prayed for the souls of men; the merchants (though in the earlier middle ages considered purely as parasites) had now the function of securing scarce commodities for society; the peasants and artisans laboured and produced the food and clothing needed for themselves and for the other sections of society. It has been shown that the contractual character of the relationships between the *upper* ranks of feudal society was often genuinely two-sided. Ecclesiastical theorists had even spoken of the *duties* of the powerful and rich towards the peasants. Now in the fourteenth century the increasing luxury of upper-class life, the immense fortunes piled up by financiers, nobles, kings and prelates on the one hand, and on the other the misery and destitution of the poor, suffering from economic crises, plagues and war, showed even to the conservative that their social ideal was far from being realised. They criticised, therefore, not to promote radical social changes, but rather to warn the rulers of the fate they were inviting if they did not mend their ways.

As for the reasons why such attacks on the sins of the great were permitted, they are easy to see. Luxurious and decadent ruling classes often enjoy being lacerated by their favourite preachers. The spectacle of a fashionable audience being attacked for its immoralities—and enjoying it—is not confined to the fourteenth century. The fashionable congregations only become indignant when their sins are recounted to others who might take action. The secret of the immunity of the majority of the fourteenth-century preachers is explained by one of the clauses of Archbishop Arundel's constitution of 1409 for the regulation of preaching. This clause states: "The preacher shall conform to his audience, otherwise he shall be punished." In other words the sins of the clergy were to be denounced only to the clergy, of the nobles only to the nobles. It was not of course the fashionable and respectable pulpit prophets such as Bromyard and Brunton against whom the constitution was directed. It was rather those who, like John Ball and some of the Lollards, denounced the sins of the rich to the poor with the object of stimulating political action.

However, it can hardly be doubted that a considerable amount of pulpit denunciation which was intended to go no further than the inculcation of seemly social behaviour must have reached ears for which it was not designed. Many of the examples and images used in the propaganda of social revolt may have come from sources where no shred of revolutionary interest can be suspected. An example of the essentially conservative type of reforming outlook is to be found in the great English poem of the period of the Revolt, William Langland's *Piers Plowman*. The hero of the poem, which is a religious allegory, is the peasant, Piers. Piers, it should be noted, is by no means a representative of the most oppressed section of the population. He is clearly one of the wealthier peasants, an employer of labour, and resentful of the day-labourer's contemporary demand for higher wages and improved conditions.

> "Labourers with no land but only their hands work
> deigned not to dine on day old vegetables;
> no penny a gallon did for them, nor a piece of bacon,
> but pork, fish or fresh flesh, fried or baked,
> and that hot and hotter for the chill of their maw.
> But he has high wages else will he chide,
> and bewail the day he ever became a working man;
> Curses the King with a will, and all his parliament,
> That makes such laws to keep the labourer down.
> But I warn you all ye workmen, earn while you can,
> Hunger is fast coming hitherward again,
> Hunger shall wake and come with floods to chasten the Wastrel."[1]

Nevertheless Langland, both in speaking directly and through the mouth of Piers, shows that he considers the toiling peasant to be the nearest to divine truth and to salvation, by the very nature of his existence. This is also characteristic of the orthodox preachers, who extol the honest toil of the countryman in contrast to the idleness of the noble, the profligacy of the rich monks and friars, the parasitism of the merchants. Against the corruption and wantonness in high places, Langland describes in detail the lives of the poor peasants, fighting for their merest existence:

> ". . . the poor in the cottage
> Charged with a crew of children and with a landlord's rent.
> What they win by their spinning to make their porridge with

[1] Quotations from *Piers Plowman* are taken from the modernised edition published in the Everyman Library.

Milk and meal, to satisfy the babes—
The babes that continually cry for food—
This they must spend on the rent of their houses,
Aye and themselves suffer with hunger,
With woe in winter rising a-nights,
In the narrow room to rock the cradle,
Carding, combing, clouting, washing, rubbing, winding, peeling rushes,
Pitiful it is to read the cottage woman's woe,
Aye and many another that puts a good face on it,
Ashamed to beg, ashamed to let neighbours know
All that they need, noontide and evening.
Many the children, and nought but a man's hands
To clothe and feed them; and few pennies come in,
And many mouths to eat the pennies up.
Bread and thin ale for them are a banquet,
Cold flesh and cold fish are like roast venison
A farthingsworth of mussels, a farthingsworth of cockles
Were a feast to them on Fridays or fast-days,
It were a charity to help these, that be at heavy charges."

In the allegorical search for Truth, Piers prescribes labour in the fields as a preparation, and, it will be noted, calls on Hunger to bring the idlers and the wastrels to heel.

It will be seen that William Langland is like the orthodox preachers, not only in the incisiveness and bitterness of his criticism of social vices, but in the essential conservatism of his outlook. Admittedly it was a conservatism of a type which would be regarded as holding little comfort for the ruling class, for it harked back to the ideal of earlier feudal society, which is contrasted with the reality of feudal society in decay. Its conservatism lay in the fact that no change in the class structure of society was envisaged.

When men and women in the course of the allegory join together to search for Truth, and are asked by Piers to engage in a sort of purification through physical labour, the noble is exempted. Says Piers:

"Surely Sir Knight, I shall toil for both of us,
And all my life will labour for love of thee,
If thou wilt keep my church and me
From the wasters and the wicked that would us destroy."

And again, Langland in speaking of those who secure God's pardon says:

"Kings and knights that holy Church defend,
Who rule the people in their realms righteously,
They have Pardon too, light purgatory,
And fellowship in paradise, with patriarchs and prophets."

Piers in his speech to the Knight implies acceptance of existing social relations—the lord's relations with his tenants, the existence of bondage—and only asks the Knight to:

"Trouble not thy tenants, save Truth assenteth,
And though ye be right to fine let mercy be your taxmaster....
Do no harm to thy bondsman, that it may be well with thee."

True, he goes on to point out that the lord's underlings may be his superiors in heaven, and here is the double edge to the social message, both of Langland and the orthodox polemists. They had no intention of upsetting the social order, only of setting it on a proper course. But the exaltation of the peasant, of the poor and of the oppressed, the threat to the powerful of heavenly vengeance, must have kindled that revolutionary sentiment which reaffirmed to the bondman his sense of his human dignity, his equality before God with all men, and made him want justice here and now, not in the life to come. We must remember that Piers the Plowman figures also in the cryptic calls to action of the revolutionary priest, John Ball.

*Unofficial Opinion*

Although the outlook of the exploited classes of feudal society was not expressed in either the romantic, the legal and philosophical, or the historical literature of the period, it is by no means without its mode of expression. Naturally there is much less of the literature of revolt than there is of the literature of the ruling class for the simple reason that the peasants who were the majority of the exploited were illiterate. Nevertheless there were many of the lower clergy who, for reasons already explained, were not only of peasant origin, but sympathetic to peasant aspirations. Some of these, like the author of *Piers Plowman,* although powerfully condemning the evils suffered by the peasantry, were unable to go further than the orthodox preachers, and emphasised the conservative doctrine of each man to his station. But others did not blunt the sharp edge of criticism with such reservations, and their contributions to the growing feeling among the peasants and artisans that they might seek a remedy through their own action must have been considerable.

It is worth noticing that most of the political songs of the late thirteenth and early fourteenth centuries which survive direct their sharpest attack against the agents of the feudal state rather than against the lords as individuals. This fits in with what we know of the events of 1381, when, although manorial records were destroyed, the individuals who suffered revolutionary justice were almost all state officials rather than manorial lords. The explanation is, of course, that not only was the coercive force of the feudal ruling class being exercised more and more by the central power, but that exploitation through national taxation, through the exaction of fines in royal courts and through the demands for bribes by a corrupt bureaucracy, was now pressing as hard or harder than the more accustomed demands for rent in money, kind or labour. Another point is that poems of social protest would in any case tend to reflect the view of the upper ranks of the peasantry, the freemen and the wealthier villeins, rather than of the lesser villeins, cottagers and wage-labourers. And it was the upper peasantry who felt the fiscal exploitation of the government more acutely than did the poor or the property-less.

Taxation and the inability to get justice without bribes—and therefore the inequality of rich and poor before the law—are the main themes of some early fourteenth-century songs. A poem in English called *Song of the Husbandman,* whilst mentioning the oppression of manorial officials such as the bailiff, the hayward and the woodward, directs its main attacks against the tax-collectors, who, in time of dearth, collect every fourth penny for the king. In order to pay his taxes, the husbandman has to prepare his poultry for the market, sell his agricultural implements, his standing corn, his seed and his cattle, and give up his year's savings in addition. As a result, his land lies uncultivated and dearth and poverty increase. Another poem of the same period, written in a mixture of French and Latin, has as its subject the evils of taxation where the point is even more strongly made that the incidence of taxation always falls on the poor, especially since the tax-collectors embezzle the proceeds. The poem goes so far as to say:

> "People are in such a plight that they can give no more. I suspect that if they had a leader, they would revolt".

Bribery and corruption are prominent themes, and sharp class feeling is expressed about this familiar consequence of bureaucracy. The poems do not only complain about the buying and selling of justice in the king's courts. They point out that because both lay and ecclesiastical judges relax the law for bribes, because the sheriffs, bailiffs, beadles, escheators and the like will take money not to do their duty, the whole weight of the bureaucratic and judicial hierarchy is felt by the poor and not by the rich. In one poem a fable is quoted in which the lion, king of the beasts, pardons the predatory fox and wolf who give him bribes from their ill-gotten spoil, but has the harmless ass torn limb from limb for eating the grass. The ass represents the poor and guileless peasant who has no money for bribes. The common conclusion of various poems on the same theme is that officials accumulate money and land from bribes and from taxes they do not hand over. Not only the poor suffer ("the poor is thus i-piled [robbed] and the riche forborne"), but the king himself is cheated, both of his taxes and of soldiers, for the officials exempt the robust from the muster of the militia for bribes, and send only the poor and weakly to the king's host.

One of the consequences of the corruption of the judiciary was that the poor man, lacking the money either to hire attorneys or to bribe the judges, was certain to suffer at the hands of law even when innocent. He was thus at the mercy of false accusers with designs on his land and goods, and since he received no protection from the law either put himself outside it or was declared an outlaw. A bitter poem entitled *The Outlaw's Song of Trailbaston* speaks of the false accusations before the venal judges on visitation, sent by the king to put down robbers and thugs (those who carried sticks or "bastons"). The author of the poem is himself falsely accused by a bench of judges touring the southern and western counties in 1305, and finds his only remedy to join others like him in the greenwood. He appeals to those who are falsely indicted to come to the "greenwood of Belregard", where there are no pleas but wild beasts and the lovely shade. Even the clerical offender, suffering from the menace of the bishop's prison, is advised to exchange such a penance for life in the woods. But the poet does not romanticise the outlaw's life, for he ends by speaking of his longing for his own country and of his wish to quit his enforced life as a robber.

The subject of outlawry, of refuge in the greenwood, brings

us to the most authentic expression in literature of the peasants themselves—the popular ballad. The poems mentioned above may have been genuine in their expression of the grievances of the exploited. They remain, however, the individual creations of literary craftsmen. Their style is even, in cases, elaborate and sophisticated. While some of the verses are in English, others are in French or Latin—languages which the people could not understand. The ballads on the other hand are wholly simple in language and form. No individual created them. They are the creations of a popular oral tradition whose poetry was not simply that of words but of song and dance. Most of them were not written down until they had passed through centuries of life on the lips of the people. The majority were committed to writing between the fifteenth and eighteenth centuries, but it is clear from their form and their content that many of them tell tales of a semi-magical character going back to tribal times; others tell stories of tragedies arising from breaches of the sacred laws of the kindred group, again bearing witness to their tribal origins; and some are tales of the struggle of the people against their feudal oppressors.

The ballads of popular resistance turn around the theme of outlawry, and the ballads of Robin Hood are the most famous of these. It has been suggested that the origins of the Robin Hood story may be found in the adventures of the outlawed followers of Simon de Montfort after their defeat and his death at the Battle of Evesham in 1265. But these men were knights and barons who were eventually received back into the king's grace. Clearly the historical origin of Robin Hood and his band of outlaws is not to be found in the single episode of the baronial wars, but in the conditions of the perpetual struggles of the peasants against their manorial lords, against the local officials of the crown and against the royal judges in whose courts they could be placed outside the law. It is in fact men such as the author of *The Outlaw's Song of Trailbaston* rather than the ambitious politicians of 1265 who are the heroes of the ballads, the songs of their own people, those who might soon have to follow them to the greenwood.

The tales of Robin Hood the outlaw were well known in the fourteenth century. They are mentioned in Langland's *Piers Plowman,* which is thought to have been written a few years before the Peasants' Rising. There are many versions of the tales known today, some of early date, some debased and of the sixteenth century or later. The finest Robin Hood story is not actually a ballad but rather an epic poem made up from the old ballads. This epic is called *A Gest of Robyn Hode* and embodies the best of the Robin Hood stories. Its social content is in no way concealed by the swiftly moving and effective narrative. The heroes are outlawed yeomen—and by that word was meant the freeborn among the peasantry. Their purpose is to rob the rich in order to give to the poor and to keep themselves alive in the process. Their particular enemies are the upper ranks of the nobility—earls, barons, archbishops, bishops and abbots. For the lesser nobility, the knights, they have no real hatred, provided the knight they encounter is a "good fellow". This leniency to the knights is probably a consequence of the peculiar situation which was characteristic of England at the end of the middle ages—a blurring of the division between the richer yeomen and the lesser gentry. The royal official, however (though drawn also from the ranks of the gentry), is the object of their most intense animosity and is typified in the ballads by the Sheriff of Nottingham, a man noted for rapacity and treachery, who meets his death at the hands of Robin Hood and his men.

As a counterpart to the hostility towards the upper ranks of society is the tenderness of the outlaws for the peasants—their own folk. Says Robin to Little John:

"... But look ye do no husband harm
That tilleth with his plough
No more ye shall no gode yeoman
That walketh by greenwood shaw ...."

This is a natural consequence of the social outlook and social origin of the outlaw. But other aspects of Robin Hood's social views are, though perhaps less expected, equally significant. Robin appears to be devout and orthodox in religion. He holds the Virgin Mary in great reverence and for her sake exempts all women from robbery on the road. Perhaps here we have an infiltration of ideas of chivalry from the literature of the upper classes. He hears mass in honour of God the Father and the Holy Ghost, as well as in honour of the Virgin. But this orthodoxy does not prevent him from despoiling the rich men of religion, especially the abbots. This is a typical fourteenth-century attitude. It was not until the fifteenth century, after the Lollards had begun to do their work, that peasant social revolt in England began to be associated with heresy.

Another feature of Robin Hood's views is important. It is his reverence for the king. This loyalty is found not only in the ballads but in the political songs, side by side with the most outspoken attacks on the lay and ecclesiastical nobility. In the *Gest of Robyn Hode* the king appears as an intermediary between the outlaws and his officials and judges, as the humorous and understanding guest in the greenwood, feasting on his own stolen deer, as the outlaws' eventual benefactor. In the political poems the king is advised to look to his evil counsellors; the author of *The Outlaw's Song of Trailbaston* curses whoever may have been responsible for the Statute of Trailbaston—"saving the king". This conception of the king's position as one above the contending classes of society was, of course, an illusion. The medieval king was the representative of the feudal nobility, of the power of the state against individual members of that class. The illusions of the peasants about the king were partly due to the fact that the king had on a number of occasions been obliged to punish the excesses of his officials, or the wielders of private jurisdiction. It must also have been fed by popular tradition from pre-feudal times, when the king was the warrior leader of a tribal society which was as yet only comparatively class-divided. The traditional illusions must have been strong, for it was loyalty to the young king Richard that disarmed the peasants in 1381, deluded as they were by his false promises of freedom. But the political conception of Wat Tyler and his comrades of a popular monarchy without nobles and without an ecclesiastical hierarchy, was the inevitable reflection of a movement that was politically immature because of its mixed and transient class basis.

In spite of illusions such as these, the popular literature of the late middle ages shows a fighting spirit such as we would expect from a peasantry which never seemed to lose courage after the many local defeats which it suffered, and which was able to gather together its experiences and its revolutionary energy for the bid for power of 1381. Robin Hood and his men deal undaunted with the Sheriff of Nottingham. Johnny Cock, a hero of the North Country, fights single-handed against the king's Seven Foresters who come to take him for poaching the king's deer. The ballad of *Adam Bell, Clim of the Clough, and William of Cloudesley* tells a tremendous story of these three outlaws fighting the whole population of Carlisle and of the exemplary end at their hands of the hated representatives of the feudal state, the king's justice and the king's sheriff.

In these relics of popular ideology we are able to see the organising power of ideas in the movement of popular revolt. The spirit of positive vigour in these fragments far outshines the more abundant sophisticated literature of chivalry of the nobility in giving the impression of great potential energy. But this, of course, is always true of the literature of revolt as compared with the literature of reaction. These songs and ballads should take their place along with John Ball's sermon, with the literature of the English Revolution, and of the modern working-class movement.

# *Part Two*

## *THE RISING*

CHAPTER FIVE

# THE FIRST OUTBREAK

THE IMMEDIATE cause of the English rising of 1381 was an attack upon the universally hated Poll Tax Commissioners now actively engaged in collecting the second part of the tax (p. 49). Riding into Brentwood came Thomas Bampton, Commissioner for the surrounding area. Commencing his investigation on May 20, he ordered the inhabitants of the villages of Fobbing, Corringham, and Stanford-le-Hope in Essex to appear before him. They came armed, refused to pay, and so forcibly did their spokesman, Thomas Baker of Fobbing, put the case of the villagers that Bampton ordered his arrest. Upon this being attempted, Bampton and his party of soldiers and clerks were attacked, stoned and driven from the village. It appears that the news was rapidly carried to London, for two London butchers, Adam Attewell and Roger Harry, set out for Essex soon after, and during May 31 and June 1 rode through all parts of the county, calling upon the people to rise.

In the meantime the men of Fobbing also called upon the people to reinforce them at Brentwood, in order that resistance could be organised against troops which the King's Council might despatch to quell the rising.

This danger soon materialised, for on June 2 Sir Robert Belknape, Chief Justice of Common Pleas, heading a contingent of troops and clerks, arrived to restore law and order. The outbreak did not seriously alarm the government, for the force was a weak one, despatched with the simple aim of hanging one or two of the ringleaders as an example, and recommencing the collection of the Poll Tax.

But the rebels were in no mood to be trifled with. They surrounded and seized Belknape and forced him to swear an oath that he would not participate in another such expedition. Then he was made to draw up a list of the justices who had convicted Poll Tax defaulters. When he had completed this, he was allowed to depart for London. The three clerks who had accompanied him received different treatment, however. They were the men who had come earlier with Bampton, and they were beheaded, as were the justices on Belknape's list as soon as they were traced.

Whilst this was taking place, the people, roused by messengers who were riding through the counties, were standing to arms, ready to prevent any action, by government officials or anyone else, against them. In Brentwood it was the arrival of the Tax Commissioner which brought them into action, whilst in Gravesend another incident provoked the people to resort to arms.

In Gravesend an official of Simon de Burley, one of the hated circle of the courtiers round the king, "a naughty man, and one contemptuous of the lowborn", arrested a citizen of Gravesend who, he claimed, was an escaped bondsman. This was an unwarranted encroachment upon the privileges of the town for Robert Belling, the arrested man, had long been a resident of Gravesend. Although Burley was out of England, the townsfolk began negotiations with the official, who demanded £300 for Belling's release and, when they demurred, ordered the arrested man to be bound and personally carried him off to Rochester Castle. As he rode forward, the townspeople rose in his wake.

By now the rebels were active in many areas. Poll Tax collectors were intercepted and attacked by armed bands, whilst Abel Ker of Erith led an attack on a monastery, after which he crossed the Thames, joined forces with another group of rebels at or near Barking, then recrossed the river with a hundred men and marched into Dartford, where the people were already astir.

Upon arriving in Dartford, Abel Ker handed over his men to Robert Cave, a master baker, who was in command of all the rebels in Dartford.

This first gathering of the rebel forces afforded the opportunity to take council and draw up plans. Following on this conference a proclamation was issued that "none that were dwelling within twelve miles of the sea should go with them, but keep the coast of the sea from enemies". Judging from this statement, it appears that the rebels had considered the possibility of a French invasion, once news of the rising reached the French coast, and they had no intention of allowing their external enemies to take advantage of the struggle. It is a pointer to the way in which the rebel forces saw their responsibilities to the country and the people.

The proclamation further declared that there were more kings than one in the land (an obvious reference to John of Gaunt) which they would not suffer, nor would they have any other for king but Richard.

Once the conference had ended and the proclamation had been made, Robert Cave and his men marched off, on June 5, to Gravesend. From there, where more men joined, the combined force marched on to Rochester Castle and began to attack it. The struggle lasted most of the day, and finally the occupants surrendered. Belling and the other prisoners were released, for the majority were not common criminals but men who had been sentenced for infringements of the Statute of Labourers or for Poll Tax evasions. In the eyes of the rebels they were political prisoners and consequently innocent.

While Rochester Castle was being stormed, fighting was going on in other parts of the county. John Legge, the man who had initiated the Poll Tax scheme, was engaged by rebels outside Canterbury and, after a brief clash, was put to flight. With Legge in retreat, the rebels then attacked a manor house owned by the Prior of the Order of St. John of Jerusalem. The Prior, Robert Hales, was Treasurer of the kingdom, and was regarded, therefore, as especially responsible for the burden of taxation. The manor house was ransacked and all the manorial rolls and records destroyed.

As the rising develops it will be noticed that, once a manor house had been stormed, the first operation undertaken by the rebels was to destroy all records of their servitude. These were in the manorial records, surveys, court rolls and bailiffs accounts, which set down, amongst other things, labour dues and every obligation owed to the lord.

The rebels were determined to banish servitude and injustice. Once victorious there would be no more serfs and consequently no further need for manorial records. Their shame and servitude were destroyed with the destruction of the rolls. It was for these reasons that the records were burned and not because, as their monk traducers would have it, the rebels were against learning and writing. Such an accusation was doubly unjust for the government had only recently promulgated a decree forbidding the spreading of learning amongst the lowly.

Most of the rebel forces were heading for Maidstone which, since June 7, had been held by the people. This town became their first headquarters—and with good reason. The two men who, above all others, inspired, shaped and led the revolt—Wat Tyler and John Ball—were both there. Ball was in Maidstone jail from which he was soon to be set free "by 20,000 men", as he had foretold when he was sentenced by Archbishop Sudbury. But first let us see what manner of man was this poor priest who became one of the earliest of the long line of English rebels.

John Ball had come to Colchester from St. Mary's in York.

From here he wandered through the countryside, for years preaching against the profligacy and corruption of the noble and rich, and calling on the peasants to end this corruption.

Another English rebel, William Morris, pictured him (in his *Dream of John Ball*) preaching on a village green:

> ". . . clad in a long dark brown gown of coarse woollen, girt with a cord, to which hung a pair of beads—or rosary as we should call it today—and a book in a bag. The man was tall and big boned, a ring of dark hair surrounded his priest's tonsure; his nose was big but clear cut with wide nostrils; his shaven face showed a longish upper lip and a big but blunt chin; his mouth was big and the lips closed firmly; a face not very noteworthy but for his grey eyes well opened and wide apart, at whiles lighting up his whole face with a kindly smile, at whiles set and stern; at whiles resting in that look as if they were gazing at something a long way off; which is the wont of a poet or enthusiast . . . and the man stood still for a while eyeing the throng. Sometimes he caught the eye of one or other and then that kindly smile spread over his face, but faded off into the sternness and sadness of a man who has heavy and great thoughts about him . . . a great expectation had fallen by now on all that throng, and no word was spoken even in a whisper, and all men's hearts and eyes were fixed upon the dark figure standing straight up now by the tall white shaft of the cross, his hands stretched out before him, one palm laid upon the other. And as for me, as I made ready to hearken, I felt a joy in my soul that I had never yet felt."

Ball's preaching made the authorities fear him, and Simon Islip, Archbishop of Canterbury, publicly excommunicated him at some date between 1362 and 1366, possibly also securing his imprisonment. Islip's successor, Simon Langham, in 1366 instructed one of the rural deans of Essex (the dean of Bocking) to threaten those who listened to Ball with excommunication, and to order Ball to appear before the archbishop for correction. Ball took no notice, and in the second year of

Simon Sudbury's pontificate (December 1376) the king, on complaint from the archbishop, issued letters patent to five commissioners from Colchester and district. They were told to arrest Ball as a contumacious excommunicate.

Whether or not this instruction was carried out, John Ball was at large on the eve of the rising, for Sudbury had to issue a writ to the officials and clergy of the diocese of Canterbury on April 26, 1381. The writ described how Ball, in spite of the earlier decrees of excommunication, had disdained to seek absolution, but had:

> "slunk back to our diocese, like the fox that evaded the hunter, and feared not to preach and argue both in the churches and church-yards (without the leave or against the will of the parochial authorities) and also in markets and other profane places, there beguiling the ears of the laity by his invectives and putting about such scandals concerning our person and those of other prelates and clergy and—what is worse—using concerning the holy father himself language such as shamed the ears of good Christians".

By this writ Sudbury ordered Ball to be publicly denounced as excommunicate, and threatened excommunication on all Ball's sympathisers. It must have been this action of Sudbury's that resulted in Ball's arrest and his consignment to the archbishop's prison in Maidstone.

The writs issued by Langham and Sudbury refer vaguely to Ball's preaching as scandalous and schismatic. But Froissart puts words into Ball's mouth which were probably near enough to what the revolutionary priest was really saying. Ball's views, as echoed by Froissart, are clearly in the tradition of the social criticism of the fourteenth-century preachers—with this essential difference: that Ball's was a call to action directed to the oppressed, not an appeal to the oppressors to mend their ways. Froissart tells us:

> "A crazy priest in the county of Kent, called John Ball, who for his absurd preaching had thrice been confined in prison

> . . . was accustomed to assemble a crowd round him in the market place and preach to them. On such occasions he would say, 'My good friends, matters cannot go well in England until all things be held in common; when there shall be neither vassals nor lords; when the lords shall be no more masters than ourselves. How ill they behave to us! For what reason do they thus hold us in bondage? Are we not all descended from the same parents, Adam and Eve? And what can they show, or what reason can they give, why they should be more masters than ourselves? They are clothed in velvet and rich stuffs, ornamented with ermine and other furs, while we are forced to wear poor clothing. They have wines, spices, and fine bread, while we have only rye, and the refuse of the straw; and when we drink, it must be water. They have handsome seats and manors, while we must brave the wind and rain in our labours in the field; and it is by our labours that they have wherewith to support their pomp. We are called slaves, and if we do not perform our service we are beaten, and we have no sovereign to whom we can complain or would be willing to hear us. Let us go to the King and remonstrate with him, he is young and from him we may obtain a favourable answer, and if not we must ourselves seek to amend our conditions.'"

It is not surprising, therefore, that the authorities hunted and imprisoned Ball, using all measures at their disposal to prevent him speaking. In particular were the upper clergy incensed since Ball advocated that no tithes should be given to them "except the party that should give the same were richer than the vicar or parson that should receive it". Their attempts to seize Ball and to silence him were of a piece with the action of the secular power. In addition to its other powers the government, by a Statute of 1361, had acquired preventive powers:

> "to restrain the evil doers, rioters and all other barrators and to pursue, arrest, take, and chastise them according to their trespass or misprision, and to cause them to be imprisoned and duly punished . . . and also to inform themselves and inquire

> touching all those who . . . go wandering and will not work as they were wont to do before this time".[1]

It is obvious that Ball fully understood why the authorities had taken action, and it is safe to surmise that it was from Maidstone Jail that Ball sent out his famous letters (fortunately they were recorded). Written in the mystical phraseology of the period (which may have had its uses for conspiratorial purposes) and steeped in religious sentiment, Ball, in rhyming couplets, calls for an armed rising of the people. Taking into account the religious sentiment and the reasons for such expression (for Ball was a man of his time) what stands out is the practical political advice contained in these letters. They reveal the mind of a mature political thinker.

The purpose of the letters was understood by the government, for a chronicler quoted by Stowe wrote that Ball had sent:

> "to the borders of the Commons in Essex a letter full of dark riddles, or dark sentences, exhorting them to proceed in their begun enterprises, which letter was after found in the pocket of one that should be hanged".

It can further be surmised from this comment that the messages were copied and distributed in various counties, for it seems unlikely that, if there were only one copy of the letter in existence, this should have remained in the pocket of a rebel after the fighting, and that this particular prisoner should have been captured with the letter on him.

The letters were, firstly, strong appeals for immediate action:

> "John Ball greeteth you all,
> And doth to understand he hath rung your bell,
> Now with right and might, will and skill,
> God speed every dell."

[1] Ed. III C.1 1361. It is interesting to note that Tom Mann, the famous working-class leader, was "preventively" imprisoned under this Statute on December 19, 1932, during the economic crisis, when the unemployed were daily becoming more militant.

This letter and one other are the only messages in which the name of Ball appears, and these must have been sent out just prior to the rising when it was no longer necessary to hide his aims. In all the other letters there runs a deeply allegorical note in which the rising is only referred to indirectly, as are the names of the leaders and their aims.

Another letter runs:

> "John Shepe, sometime St. Mary priest of York, and now in Colchester, greeteth well John Nameless and John Miller and John Carter, and biddeth them that they beware of guile in borough and standeth together in God's name and biddeth Pierce Plowman to go to his work and chastise well Hob the Robber, and take with him John Trueman and all his fellows and no more, and look that ye shape to one head and no more."

John Shepe must have been an assumed name of John Ball, since the description is of himself.

The letter is a definite instruction for action. He names various men, probably by their assumed names since it was possible that the letter would fall into the hands of the authorities, and bids them beware of betrayal, "guile in borough". Then he bids the rebels to stand firm, "standeth together in God's name," and to proceed with their noble work (here he uses the symbolic name of Piers Plowman, the redeemer in Langland's poem) of settling accounts with their oppressors. He specifically names Sir Robert Hales, the Treasurer of the Government, "Hob the Robber", as one needing the close attention of the rebels, since Hales was the man most concerned with the collection of taxes. Then follows some very necessary advice—"and look that ye shape to one head and no more", for there must be discipline in a rebellion. It would be fatal to have conflicting and confusing orders. One leader is the definite advice. Furthermore, the letter continues, only reliable men should undertake the necessary task—"take with him John Trueman and all his fellows and no more".

Time and time again this theme runs through the letters: Select your men. Close your ranks. Look to one head and no more and, once you have chosen him, trust him, and once you have started the rising, then prosecute it with the greatest vigour.

> "Jack Carter prays you all that ye make good end of what ye have begun and doeth well and aye better and better."

So might it be said in modern terms, "audacity, audacity, and again audacity".

The only other letter which mentions John Ball runs:

> "John Ball, St. Mary Priest greeteth well all manner of men and biddeth them in the name of the Trinity, Father, Son and Holy Ghost, stand manlike together in truth, and help truth, and truth shall help you:
>
> Now reigneth price in price,
> Covetise is holden wise,
> Lechery without shame,
> Gluttony without blame,
> Envy reigneth with reason
> And sloth is taken in great season.
> God do bote [exact the penalty] for now is time."

The theme is obvious, and is as urgent a call for action as the first letter in which Ball openly calls for rebellion. His letters return again and again to this theme.

> "Jack Trueman [runs another letter] doeth you to understand that
> Falseness and guile hath reigned too long
> And truth hath been set under a lock
> And falseness reigneth in every flock,
> No man may come truth to
> But he must sing fi dedero.[1]

[1] Evidently an allusion to the vested interests of the Church.

Speak, spend and speed, quoth John of Bathom[1]
And therefore sin fareth as wild flood,
True love is away that was so good
God do bote for now is time."

There is no longer any truth or justice in the land. We have allowed such things to continue too long, and the Church is just as corrupt as the rest. Only the common people can set things right ("John Trueman and his fellows").

"John Miller asketh help to turn his mill right:
He hath ground small, small,
The King's Son of Heaven will pay for it all,
Look the mill go right, with its four sails dight.
With right and with might, with skill and with will,
And let the post stand in steadfastness,
Let right help might, and skill go before will,
Then shall our mill go aright.
But if might go before right, and will go before skill
Then is our mill mis-a-dight.
Beware ere ye be woe.
Know your friend from your foe
Take enough and cry Ho!
And do well and better and flee from sin,
And seek out peace and dwell therein,
So biddeth John Trueman and all his friends."

These were the letters and the theories of this English rebel leader who had been released from Maidstone Jail by the people he had served so well.

It is also at Maidstone that Wat Tyler is first recorded in history. Little is known of his origins or early life, but in his last nine days this man led the forces which shook the very foundations of the State. He is recognised as the leader and spokesman during two vitally important conferences with Richard II.

Tyler, too, came from Colchester, the home of John Ball, and it would seem likely that he had been influenced by the

[1] A bishop.

preaching of Ball. As well as being a capable leader of men, Tyler was also a powerful speaker, an able negotiator, and seemingly a good military strategist. It is said that he had seen active service in France and had learned his military skill there. Even his most bitter enemies, the monks who wrote the contemporary chronicles, refer to him as a "crafty fellow of an excellent wit, but lacking grace", and "endowed with great intelligence if only it had been applied to a rightful purpose". This has inspired a modern historian, Sir Charles Oman, to write that Tyler was "a quick-witted, self-reliant, ambitious fellow with an insolent tongue and the gift of magniloquence which a mob orator needs".

There is no record of Tyler's leadership being questioned or challenged, although he was a strict disciplinarian, putting to death any of the rebels caught looting. He was firm, clear-headed and full of commonsense. He was held in such esteem by the rebels that they swore that only the laws issued by him would be accepted as valid and obeyed by them. Thus they put him on a level with the king, who alone could issue laws, with the consent of Parliament. Tyler's name was used by other rebel leaders as an earnest of their authority and they carried out their tasks under his instructions. Before any decisive step was taken by Grindcobbe at St. Albans, for example, Tyler's advice and consent was first sought and obtained.

Not only did the rebel army place Tyler at their head in Maidstone, but they also issued a statement which proclaimed:

1. Continued allegiance to King Richard and the commons.
2. That they would accept no king named John.[1]
3. To agree to no tax that might be levied henceforth in the kingdom; no consent to any except it were a fifteenth.
4. To be ready whenever they were called upon.

[1] This was directed against Gaunt, self-styled King of Castile.

Gaunt was the enemy; he was the personification of all that against which they had risen. The programme they issued at Maidstone was an attack upon power, privilege, misrule and corruption. It called for the defence of the rights of the common people. The young king, rid of all evil council, would from henceforth rule in the interest of the people. They were determined to break the chains which bound them to the soil, whilst all men who enforced the power of Gaunt were to be put to death.

Careful note had been kept of all the state officials and others concerned in the oppression of the people, and those who played an active part in it were to be put to death. It should be stressed that there was no wanton massacre by the rebel army. All those put to death were executed for past misdeeds, of which the rebels had long records.

With the conclusion of all business at Maidstone, Tyler went into action. Placing himself at the head of a body of men, he led them to Canterbury, the most important political centre in Kent. Here it was that pilgrims from all parts foregathered to pay homage at the tomb of Thomas a Becket. Canterbury joined wholeheartedly with the rebels. Upon their arrival the entire town turned out to welcome Tyler and his band, but after courtesies had been exchanged the men rode on to the seat of Archbishop Sudbury, who was also Chancellor, the highest official of the state.

The Palace was thoroughly searched and all documents, rolls and records were heaped together, set alight and completely destroyed. The work was carried out with extreme thoroughness and rough good humour. The rebels walked through chambers and corridors full of rich tapestry and finely carved furniture. Froissart reports one of them as having said: "The Chancellor of England has had this piece of furniture very cheap. Now he must give us an account of his revenue, and of the very large sums which he has levied since the coronation of this king."

With this task completed, Tyler proceeded to the Cathedral. Interrupting a Mass, for he had a very important pronouncement to make, he informed the monks and the congregation that they were to elect a new Archbishop. Sudbury had been condemned to death as a traitor, and would shortly be executed, he announced.

Tyler's statement leads to the belief that this step had been decided upon at Maidstone, for the election of a new Archbishop was one of the chief demands of the rebels, who were church reformers of a very advanced kind and, as will be seen later, proposed to the king some extremely radical changes in the role which the church would play in the new state. The office of Archbishop was one of the highest in the land and would, therefore, have to be filled by one in whom the people had the greatest confidence. In all probability it had been decided at Maidstone that John Ball was to fill this honourable office, for at Blackheath, after he had preached to them, the rebel army raised a shout that they would have no one but him for Archbishop. Tyler's announcement from the pulpit at Canterbury Cathedral was the first intimation to the country that the rebels intended to change the structure and leadership of England.

Once he had stated the decision of the rebels, Tyler withdrew from the Cathedral and rode back to the centre of the town. Here, before the assembled citizens, the mayor and bailiffs solemnly accepted the programme and principles of the rebels, swearing an oath of loyalty to "Richard and the True Commons". Canterbury had the honour of being the first town in the country to accept the rule of the rebel army, and to undertake to administer the town according to their principles.

Upon conclusion of the various ceremonies Tyler rejoined

the main force waiting in Maidstone, and from there they marched back to Rochester, where a welcome similar to that of Canterbury was given to them. At Rochester, Sir John Newton, chief jailer of Rochester Castle, together with several other noblemen, was taken as a hostage and forced to accompany the rebel forces to Blackheath. It was only the men, and not their families, who were taken prisoner. Even the family of John of Gaunt was allowed to go unharmed, although some of his administrators were attacked by the rebels.[1]

1 "They wrought much damage in Kent, and notably to Thomas Hazelden, a servant of the Duke of Lancaster, because of the hate that they bore to the said duke. They cast his manors to the ground and all his houses, and sold his beasts, his horses, his good cows, his sheep and pigs, and all his store of corn at a cheap price," states the *Anonimale Chronicle*. Thus even Gaunt's property was not looted, but his corn and cattle sold to the peasants at a fair price. This again shows the discriminatory character of the rebels' actions.

CHAPTER SIX

# BLACKHEATH AND LONDON

On Wednesday, June 12, the rebel army reached Blackheath and pitched camp. Here they were joined by many rebel bands from outlying areas, who had hastened to join the main forces once the news had reached them. From Blackheath a company of rebels were detailed to proceed to the Marshalsea and King's Bench prisons, situated in Southwark. Both these prisons were stormed and, after the prisoners had been released, burned to the ground. Again this was an understandable act, for the prisons of Marshalsea and King's Bench were infamous ones to which were sent offenders who had broken the Statute of Labourers.

From Southwark the rebels marched to Lambeth and destroyed the palace of the Archbishop, since it was the property of a traitor whom Tyler had denounced in Canterbury Cathedral.

So were the torches of rebellion lit. To the commons of London they were signals heralding freedom; but to the youthful king and the court grouped round him they were fearful portents.

With the rebel army so close to its walls, London was again in a ferment. The apprentices, journeymen and certain of the master-craftsmen were preparing to help the rebels on the outskirts of the city, whilst the supporters of the King's Council were making hasty preparations to repel the attack. Previously the city poor had fought bravely to maintain the rights and interests of their masters. They had been only a mob of apprentices and journeymen, fighting for whichever group of masters paid the most, but for some time now there had been a change. It has been noted already (p. 17) that they had begun to see that the interests of the masters were not their interests.

Therefore the London artisans made common cause with the rebel peasants, and planned to force the city gates from within to enable the rebel army to enter without fighting. The city walls and gates were the main bastion of defence and would be closely guarded and watched by the other side. In London that task was placed in the hands of one Walworth, Lord Mayor of London, speculator and brothel keeper[1] and one of the most powerful members of the Fishmongers' Gild.

Walworth carried out the task with characteristic vigour. London was divided into wards over which the aldermen had control—each alderman being responsible for a given ward. He had seen to it that the members of his own and other victuallers' gilds held these important political posts, and among these aldermen were Walter Sybyle, William Tonge and John Horn. These men appear to have had earlier links with the rebels and, by accident or design, although later events point to the latter, they were given control over the wards responsible for guarding the main gates of the city. These were the Bridge Ward, where the fishmongers held sway, and Ald Gate, the district of the butchers and poulterers. It is mainly due to the actions of these aldermen that the rebels were able to enter the city of London without a blow being struck in its defence.

Walworth sent a representative and responsible group of citizens, consisting of Alderman Horn, Adam Carlyll and John Fresh, to Blackheath to warn the rebel army not to approach London which, he threatened, would be stoutly defended. Horn managed by some means to slip away and in a quick talk with Tyler told him to advance swiftly since

[1] He held the monopoly of the London brothels, many of which were situated in Walworth and Southwark.

all was in readiness for them. He must have told him that the whole of London was behind the rising and that when the rebel army marched into London "they would be lovingly received in the city, as a father by his children, or as a friend by his friend", as the Sheriff's inquiry into the evidence against Horn and his colleagues later stated.[1]

Horn stayed with the rebel army until nightfall, and then smuggled into the city three of the rebels, whom he sheltered in his house. There they met some of their London supporters and the final plans were drawn up. Leaving the rebels in conference, Horn rode to the Lord Mayor. Arriving here, he said he had spoken to the rebels, but despite the Mayor's warning, which he had personally conveyed, the rebel forces were determined to march on London. But, he added, Walworth need have no fear for the city. He swore by his head that the rebels would do neither harm nor damage.

The next day, Thursday, June 13, was Corpus Christi, a day of solemn festival, and the camp was up early to hear Mass celebrated by John Ball. When he mounted the pulpit he saw before him, drawn up in battle array with the two great standards at their head, a great body of men. Most of these had stormed castles and manor houses, almost barehanded. Now, near the journey's end, they were praying for the successful ending of the enterprise they had begun.

Ball's sermons had little to do with religion, despite his religious analogies. To the assembled forces he made a clear and detailed statement in the course of which he very pointedly recapitulated the views held by the rebels, and their aims. The rebel forces were on the eve of their most serious engagement. They were about to attack the City of London—a city in which were concentrated most of the retinue of the crown.

[1] From this it appears obvious that the amount of support the rebels had amongst Londoners was imposing. Sufficient certainly to have impressed Horn and his friends. The extent of this support can be judged from the later attitude towards the peasants when they entered the city.

Apart from the fighting which might have to be faced, despite the promise of the aldermen, there would be frenzied attempts on the part of the authorities to side-track the peasants with false promises. Together with this there was the danger of the intimidation which the ruling class could bring to bear because of their great wealth and power, which they knew how to exploit to the full.

In order to face this successfully the rebels must be sure of what had to be done to win their demands. A certain number of rebels may have understood this, for Ball and his friends had long been preaching in the villages and towns, but in this assembly there were many who did not know; who had only recently been drawn into the struggle and saw in it an opportunity to obtain redress for their grievances. Therefore now was the time to explain to the largest number of rebels gathered at Blackheath what was meant by the social and political criticism which had for so long been preached. It was very necessary to do this for now they were going to put it into practice.

Ball gave as his text the old rhyme which summed up so well all that for which he had been fighting these thirty years:

> "When Adam delved and Eve span
> Who was then the gentleman?"

and

> "by the word of that proverb which he took for his theme, to introduce and prove, that from the beginning all men were made alike by nature, and that bondage and servitude was brought in by oppression of naughty men against the will of God. For if it had pleased God to have made bondsmen he would have appointed them from the beginning of the world, who should be slave and who lord. They sought to consider, therefore, that now was a time given to them by God, in the which, laying aside the continual bondage, they might if they would, enjoy their long wished for liberty. Wherefore, he admonished them, that they should be wise and after the manner of a good

husbandman that tilled his ground, and did cut away all noisome weeds that were accustomed to grow and oppress the fruit, they should make haste to do now at this present the like.

"First the Archbishop and great men of the kingdom were to be slain; after, lawyers, justices, lastly whomsoever they knew like hereafter to be hurtful to the Commons, they should dispatch out of the land, for so might they purchase safety to themselves hereafter, if the great men being once taken away, there remained amongst them equal liberty, all one nobility, and like authority and power."[1]

Maybe to many of those present a great deal of this was inexplicable, but they understood enough to make them shout aloud in support of Ball. According to the Sheriff's inquiry it made "the common people to esteem of him in such a manner" that they cried out "he should be Archbishop of Canterbury and Chancellor of the realm, for he only deserved the honour".

It is obvious that Ball gave full vent to ideas which were so often heard in the fourteenth century, but which he had developed and carried much further than any other man of that time. With his opening sentences he put forward the revolutionary idea of equality, thereby challenging the entire conception of the feudal church and state. Not only did he challenge the prevailing ideology, but he gave his conception of how the divisions in society arose—by the action of evil men who robbed, exploited and built up their wealth and power by means of oppression. If God had intended that there should be two classes in society—lord and serf, exploiters and exploited—then these two classes would have existed from the creation of the world. But this was not so, for the Bible said that in the beginning there were only workers. Adam delved and Eve span—both equal before the eyes of God.

It was this conception of equality which the ruling class of

[1] The speech is reported in the contemporary *Chronicon Anglie*, and the translation quoted is by the sixteenth-century historian, John Stowe.

that day could not grasp. It was beyond their understanding why the very basis of their society, the rock upon which their system was founded—that of service to the overlord—should be questioned. Even the king could not approach God as an equal although he was semi-divine. The king had to approach his Creator through the offices of a mediating clergy. The whole thing was incomprehensible and there was only one answer. The man was mad, and his aim was to destroy society, to turn the country into a wilderness. It was this belief that caused the anguished cry of the Earl of Salisbury, which Froissart records:

> "If the rebels are successful . . . then . . . it will be all over with us and our heirs, and England will be a desert."

Like the sermon summarised by Froissart, John Ball's sermon at Blackheath is an exposition of class struggle in England. But it goes further than that. In the earlier sermon Ball had suggested that the people go to the king to redress their wrongs. Now they were going. This sermon was therefore a call for action—a call to the peasants to see that they were not fobbed off, but that their demands were granted.

With the Mass concluded, a meeting of the rebel leaders was held, at which a message was drafted and sent to the king by one of the hostages. Alderman Horn, who had with him the Royal Standard, was present. He told the Council that all was ready.

> "Come to London," he said, according to the Sheriff's inquiry, "we are all to a man your friends, and ready to act with you as you have suggested, and show you obedience."

The message which the hostage took to the king stated in bold terms that they, the rebels, were acting only in the interests of the king. The kingdom had for years been misgoverned, to the great dishonour of the realm, and to the great oppression of the people, both by the king's uncle—John of Gaunt—and by the clergy, more especially by the Archbishop of Canterbury, from whom they were determined to have an account of his ministry.

As soon as the hostage, a knight, entered the Tower, he was ushered into the presence of the king and the court. The group round the throne included the Lord Mayor and other merchant princes, who were anxiously awaiting further news of the rising. The principal ministers were there, as well as the king's mother. She had been captured by the rebels at Eltham, but she had been allowed to pass through their ranks, under the direct protection of Wat Tyler, who promised that no harm should befall her.

The knight was most abject in his apologies. He was, he hastened to assure the court, a prisoner of the rebel army. The court, however, was in no mood for these formalities. "Tell us what you are charged with, we hold you excused," came the sharp request. The knight then gave the essence of the message, and added:

> "They wish to have no-one but yourself, and you need not fear for your person, as they will not do you the least harm; they have always respected you as their king, and will continue to do so; but they desire to tell you many things which they say is necessary that you should hear."

The favourable report of the knight somewhat calmed the fear of the Council, and, after a brief conference, it was decided to allow the king to meet the rebels. The message had given them a measure of reassurance, for if the rebels still believed that the king was a neutral factor, then there was still a chance of survival. Belief in the king was the one straw which they could grasp. The rising had spread rapidly, engulfing them before they could collect their wits. Never had they been so terrified, for suddenly, seemingly from nowhere, had sprung a rebel army, well led, with a programme of demands. The King's Council had been entirely unaware of the danger. They had thought they knew every move and whisper of the serfs; they were aware of the discontents, of the "confederacies", of the "scandals" and "false rumours" which were spread about the "great ones of the land", but they obviously had no idea of the extent of such a move amongst the peasants. A rising had been organised under their very noses, and they had been unaware of it. They could understand the sudden flare-up of a few hundred peasants or artisans, for this was a common occurrence; such riots could be easily crushed. But this was something different, the lower orders were seemingly rising in one mass. A few years previously the French peasantry, the Jacquerie, had risen, and had wrought great slaughter amongst the nobility before the rising had been suppressed. Were they in turn to go through a similar ordeal?

The court must have realised by now that there was no body of men upon whom they could, at that moment, rely. Even if there were among them a few men with the courage and determination to try and muster forces from the countryside, it was obviously impossible to break through the rebel lines which, by now, had cut off London. The Council, therefore, hastily grasped this faint hope which the rebels' message contained to sustain them in the swift tides of rebellion.

It should be made clear that at no time did the king play an independent part during the ensuing proceedings, or throughout the whole course of the rising. This point is emphasised for, as the struggle grew sharper, the more did it revolve round the person of King Richard II, who was both a minor and a weakling. He was under the direct control of the King's Council which consisted of, amongst others, Sudbury, the Archbishop of Canterbury and Chancellor, and Sir Robert Hales, the Treasurer.

These men, together with the king's mother, who was his

guardian (and not the sort of woman to allow herself to be ignored), ruled England. She played her part in influencing the fifteen-year-old king, who had never at any time shown any desire to assert his independence. Neither before nor after the legendary speeches and heroic deeds ascribed to him by Froissart and the monks did he ever show any signs of courage or clear-sighted action; nor did he demand his independence from the King's Council.

"It is somewhat strange," wrote Bishop Stubbs in his *Constitutional History of England,* "that King Richard, after he had given proof of his ability, was content to remain for some years longer in tutelage," or, in less polite words, willing to be tied to the apron-strings of his mother. No matter how hard Froissart and the other contemporary chroniclers try to build him up as a brave and courageous figure, they cannot camouflage his weakness. "Neither by natural disposition nor youthful training was he fitted to come through the troubles bequeathed to him by his grandfather," says Professor James Tait:

> "Abrupt and stammering in speech, hasty and subject to sudden gusts of passion . . . the somewhat unmanly despair attributed to him . . . may not be out of keeping with his character. He was vain and fond of fine things . . . one of his coats was valued at 30,000 marks. . . . In later years he was charged with turning night into day with drinking bouts and with indulging in unnatural vice. . . ."

It is upon this neurotic that the historian has had to drape the mantle of heroism. His weak and vicious character cannot be hidden, despite the whitewash so liberally spread.

All the unwonted activity shown by the king during the rising was due to the responsible ministers thrusting him forward because of the loyal sentiments professed by the rebels. The Council naturally prompted the king, and carefully went over with him all that he had to do and say. There was little loyalty one to the other, for when the rebels demanded the heads of certain ministers these were hurriedly abandoned to their fate, even though they were members of the King's Council, so that the lives of the rest might be spared. The king alone was their sheet anchor, so they pushed him into the limelight, controlling him from the shadow.

Later that day the king stepped into his barge, and was rowed downstream to Rotherhithe, where the rebel forces awaited him. At the sight of the royal barge, which contained not only the king but some of the hated ministers, the rebels burst out into wild shouting. Intermingled with their demands, they shouted threats to the ministers. Their aggressive demeanour and their shouting so frightened the king and his advisors that they gave immediate orders for the barge to be kept in midstream. Upon reaching safety, the king asked what his people wanted. He had come to hear what they had to say. In reply the rebels asked that the king should first land, then they would discuss their grievances with him. This demand caused still greater concern amongst the ministers, for to allow the king to be separated from them meant suicide. Hurriedly the Earl of Salisbury rose to his feet. Erect and with full dignity he cried: "Gentlemen, you are not properly dressed, nor are you in fit condition for a king to talk with." Froissart, who recorded this scene, adds that nothing more was said on either side!

With the failure of the Rotherhithe meeting, if it can be dignified by such a name, the rebels saw that only with the capture of London could the King's Council be brought to reason. The Essex rebels were on the north side of the river and were probably in sight of the rebel forces on the Kent side. Horn's insistent demands that they march into London, as well as the craven behaviour of the king and the ministers on the barge, had its effect and the rebels began to stream towards London.

They made for London Bridge, attacking and burning on their way Walworth's brothels, which he had hired to Flemish prostitutes. When the Lord Mayor saw so fruitful a source of his income destroyed, his wrath rose higher than the flames. It inspired him and some of his fellow merchants to attempt a still firmer stand against the rebel forces.

At the approach of the peasants, Alderman Walter Sybyle, a member of the Fishmongers' Gild and Alderman of the Bridge, which he had occupied with his men that morning, made preparations to admit them to London. He prevented all attempts to defend the bridge, and resisted the placing of armed guards, turning them back, reads the indictment,

> "with insult and contumely, openly declaring these men of Kent are our friends and the king's".

The outraged merchants told Sybyle of the attacks on the prisons and the burning of the Lord Mayor's brothels, but the Alderman was unmoved. "What of that?" he answered. "It has been merited for twenty years past."

Finally because of the determined stand of the Londoners, whose threatening behaviour alarmed Walworth, the Lord Mayor came to an understanding with Wat Tyler that the rebels would pay for all they took and do no damage. With the acceptance of these terms, the rebel army marched into London. It had fallen without a blow being struck, owing to the intense class and factional divisions, and the chaos now existing in the ranks of the ruling class.

In the meantime Thomas Farringdon, a citizen of London, had attached himself to the Essex rebels. Under his guidance they entered London through the Ald Gate, almost at the same time as the Kent rebels were pouring into London over London Bridge. The strength of the opposition to the Mayor and the ruling class can be gauged by the fact that Walworth had ordered the closing and barring of the Ald Gate a day earlier but, despite these orders, the gate was unbarred and flung open by Alderman Tonge at the approach of the men of Essex. Farringdon appears to have been exceedingly active throughout the rising. He assisted the rebel leaders to draw up a list of traitors who were to be condemned and, the day after the rebels had captured London, accompanied Jack Straw and a band of rebels to Highbury, where the great manor of Sir Robert Hales ("Hob the Robber", mentioned in one of Ball's letters) stood. This manor, together with others of his residences, was destroyed.

The rebels entered London in disciplined ranks. Many towns and villages were represented by contingents of men organised in their own companies.

> "They entered in troops," recorded Froissart, "of one or two hundred, by twenties or thirties, according to the populousness of the towns they came from."

Everything was conducted in a quiet and orderly fashion. Even the most hostile chroniclers admit that there was no looting or irresponsible behaviour. Supplies placed at the disposal of the rebels were bought and paid for, according to the agreement reached between Tyler and Walworth. The dignity and bearing of the men compelled admiration from all onlookers, who gave them as warm a welcome as did the men of Canterbury to Wat Tyler and his troops. Apprentice, journeyman and small merchant combined to give welcome to this army with freedom emblazoned on its standards. Once the men had been lodged, sections, led by Londoners, marched off to their appointed tasks.

The greatest number of rebels marched along the Strand to the Savoy Palace, the residence of the most hated man in the land—John of Gaunt—the recognised leader of the most reactionary group of speculators, financiers and corrupt barons, which was bleeding the country. It was well for Gaunt that he was absent in Scotland and that his sense of caution kept him there. He remained on the Scottish borderland, allowing his inheritance to be taken from him without attempting to strike a blow for its retention. Wherever his property stood, bands of rebels burned and destroyed it, distributing his lands and cattle.

The Savoy Palace had just been completed. There was no residence in England to compare with it in beauty and stateliness, nor was there any other residence which so symbolised the oppression against which the people had risen. Before the work of destruction began, two things were done. Firstly the family of Gaunt was allowed to depart. They went unharmed through the ranks of rebels, who had no quarrel with these. Their fight was with the "great ones of the land". Secondly a stern warning was issued to all ranks by the rebel leaders. Lest it might appear to others outside London, and those not yet with the rebels, that the burning of the Savoy was a matter of wanton destruction for loot and plunder, the following declaration was made:

> "That none, on pain to lose his head, should presume to convert to his own use anything that there was or might be found, but that they should break such plate and vessels of gold and silver, as were in that house in great plenty, into small pieces, and throw the same into the Thames or into privies. Clothes of gold and silver and silk and velvet they should tear; rings and jewels set with precious stones they should break in mortars, that the same might be of no use."

The order was carried out to the letter. One man caught putting a piece of silver-plate in his breast was taken and thrown to the flames. "We be zealous of truth and justice," said these ancestors of the Levellers and Chartists, "and not thieves and robbers." A group of men who entered the wine cellars and drank themselves unconscious were not rescued but were allowed to burn to death.

Historians anxious to blacken the rebels have searched the records to try to find details of looting and plundering but have found only one indictment, which accused the prisoner of stealing some gold from the palace.

Having destroyed the Savoy Palace, the rebels returned to the Temple, which was not only the home of the lawyers but also the property of "Hob the Robber". Within the Temple "lurked the lawyers, like rats and evil spirits" guarding the rolls and records which helped to ruin honest men. Every charter and roll was torn and burned. Tax records, royal accounts, book-chests and furniture, all were cast into the fire that blazed in the Middle Temple.

The next places to be burned were the Fleet and Newgate prisons. Westminster prison had already been destroyed. They were mostly used for the imprisonment of peasants and artisans who had infringed the Statute of Labourers, and their destruction was as much a political act as the burning of the Savoy Palace.

From the Fleet prison the rebels marched to the Tower. Here, guarded by 600 men-at-arms, were the king and the King's Council. A great part of the rebel army had decided to bivouack there and were feeding on provisions intercepted whilst being taken into the Tower. They stayed in the precincts not because they could find no resting place in the city but because here were their chief enemies.

CHAPTER SEVEN

# TWO MEETINGS

WHILST THE rebel army was surrounding the Tower, two meetings were being held. The rebel leaders had met at the house of Thomas Farringdon, where plans for future action were discussed. At this meeting, obviously, the terms which were to be put to the king were discussed, since insistent demands were being made for an interview with him. Here too, possibly, the list of men to be condemned was drawn up, containing such names as John of Gaunt, Sudbury, Hales, Courtney, Thomas Bampton, Belknape and John Legge, the King's Sergeant, the man responsible for the Poll Tax Collectors.

For the rebels it was a victory meeting. London had fallen without a struggle. But it was too successful, for had there been a hitch, had there been hard fighting, then the rebels would not have allowed the initiative to pass from their hands to the king. Before entry into London they waited to be received by the king at Rotherhithe, and after the craven behaviour of the king and Council they had no choice but to march on London. Now London was in their hands, the king and his court besieged, the armed forces scattered. England was in the hands of the rebels; yet they waited until word was received from the king, granting them an audience, before they placed their demands before him.

What may have been in the minds of the more astute of the rebels—and later events underline this supposition—was that the king exercised supreme authority because of the authority and power vested in kingship. If the king were once won over to their side, or even coerced over, then submission of the nobility and obedience of the others would be obtained the more readily and easily. Armed with the authority of the king's seal, it would be easier to break down opposition, to control the nobility, to overcome the barriers which would be placed in their path by the Church. This is what actually happened when the king, advised by the King's Council, put his seal to the charters of freedom distributed at Mile End. Therefore the goodwill of the king was earnestly sought by the rebels.

The demands of the rebels, drafted on Thursday, June 13, in order to be placed before the king at the earliest possible moment, were:

(1) that all men should be free from servitude and bondage so that thenceforth there should be no bondsmen;
(2) that the king should pardon all men of what estate soever, all manner of action and insurrections committed and all manner of treasons, felonies, transgressions and extortions by any of them done, and to grant them peace;
(3) that all men might thenceforth be enfranchised to buy and sell in every county, city, borough, town, fair, market and other place within the realm of England;
(4) that no acre of land holden in bondage or service should be holden out but for fourpence and if it had been holden for less aforetime, it should not be hereafter enhanced.

It is necessary to give careful consideration to these important social and economic demands. Firstly they show above all that the rebels were not boorish ruffians but capable and responsible men who were well aware of the economic and political ills affecting their country. Secondly they reveal the main economic ideas and demands which were the motivating forces of the rebellion. Briefly the demands were: freedom from serfdom; freedom of trade; cheap land; and common justice.

The first proposal meant the abolition of serfdom. By granting it the king freed his subjects from all manner of bondage and servitude. The serf was to be manumitted. He was no longer to be bound to the soil or subject in all things to the will of the lord, and was to have full legal rights against him. It had long been established that the freeman had legal rights against his lord in the royal courts. It abolished all forms of servile labour, whether it was week work, harvest work, or any other form of labour rendered either by a freeman or serf.

The second proposal was an obvious one. The rebels asked the king to give his assurance that he would not prosecute or take any action against the rebels, but would make the rising legal by granting his peace to all those connected with it.

Thirdly comes the proposal that the freed serf be given the right to buy and sell, free of tax, in all cities, boroughs, markets, fairs and other places. It should be noted that borough privileges were specifically directed against the peasants and other agricultural producers with the object of making the terms of trade between town and country unfavourable to the country.

The fourth demand, which contained the proposal for the regulation of the price of land at 4d. per acre was in effect a demand of the poor peasant for his holding to be freed of all the customary dues and services which burdened it. He wanted the king to commute all these to an all-inclusive rate of 4d. per acre. The rents up to 2s. per acre, which were paid by the richer peasant, were leasehold rents—"economic rents"—and it is more than likely that the rich peasant, who also took an active part in the rising, took advantage of this move to try to lower the rent of his leasehold land.

These, then, were the demands which the rebels were determined to present to the king and to carry out as speedily as possible, once the agreement of the king was obtained. But whilst these earnest and thoughtful men were drafting these demands which would, if granted, have created a new society, however unconscious they were of the fact, the second meeting, the King's Council, was holding its deliberations within the walls of the besieged Tower of London.

At this Council two points of view were being fiercely debated. One, proposed by the brutal Walworth and representing the City interests, was filled with the impatience of action. Crude and rough, without that finesse and subtlety which can only be acquired after long experience of power and rule, he wanted to teach "these shoe-less ruffians" a lesson. Whilst they were asleep, he argued, he and the loyal men-at-arms would make a surprise sally and strike terror into the ranks of this mob sleeping round their camp fires. He could guarantee a force of between six and seven thousand armed men, which would include most of the merchants and their households. This was his plan. The burning of the brothels had fired his blood. Only slaughter could avenge his lost profits.

Against him argued the Earl of Salisbury, a mature statesman, and his plan bore the hallmark of ruling-class craft and diplomacy. It was based on the inexperience of the people in the ways of their rulers. If we sally forth now, commented Salisbury on Walworth's proposal, we may have a momentary success. But, when the first alarm dies down and the peasants re-form their ranks, what then? What if the fighting spreads into the streets, away from the Tower, and reinforcements come to the aid of the rebels? He may have reminded the Council of the fighting qualities of the Londoners when their smaller privileges had been threatened, and when even John of Gaunt had had to fly for his life. That was fierce enough, even with a small number involved. Now practically the entire population of London appeared to be supporting the rebels. Therefore this was decidedly not the moment to strike their blow. "Besides," he added in a passage already referred to (p. 113), "if we begin what we cannot carry through, we should never be able to repair matters. It will be all over with us and our heirs, and England will be a desert."

This grave warning to the assembled Council emphasised the dangerous position in which they were placed. They knew that temporarily the rebels were in the saddle, and Salisbury's plan made a strong appeal because it offered so many variations and did not expose them to swift counter-attack. First try to get them home, argued Salisbury. If that fails, try negotiating, drawing this out as long as possible so that the faint-hearted would begin to drift home. Use fair words, and when the negotiations have gone on long enough, grant some of the requests, so that again the more easily satisfied might break away and go back to their villages. Then, when the vigilance of the rebels is at its lowest, and when their aims have become divided and the unity of purpose weakened, then is the time to strike.

Salisbury's policy carried the day, and an immediate attempt was made to get the rebels to go home. It is quite possible that some members of the King's Council felt that if they gave way immediately to the rebel demand that the king attend in person to hear their grievances, they would be lowering the prestige of the crown; that once an interview had been granted it would mean that the king had surrendered to mob-violence and that it admitted implicitly that the rebels had a case to state. It would mean that some immediate concessions would have to be granted, and that might be a bad thing. Yet, whatever their qualms, they felt that Salisbury's counsel was the wisest.

The king mounted a turret on the east side of the Tower. He faced what is now St. Catherine's Dock, where the main body of the rebels lay. Speaking as by rote, he began by promising them his forgiveness for all they had done if they would now peacefully disperse to their homes.

This request enraged the rebels. It was not this that they

expected to hear from a beleaguered king. Back came an answering roar that they would never leave until the traitors in the Tower were secure, nor would they move one step until all the demands upon their charter had been granted, which demands they chanted in mighty chorus. Urgently prompted from the rear, the king melodramatically drew up and sealed a charter in their sight and, calling upon two knights, he commanded them to carry the charter to the people. Standing upon an old chair, one of them solemnly unrolled the document and read it to the rebels:

> "The king thanks his good Commons for their loyalty and pardons all their illegal offences, but he wishes every one to return home and set down his grievances and send them to him. By the advice of his lords he will then provide such remedy as will be profitable to himself, his Commons, and the whole realm."

The effect was electrical. Roused to fury by the arrogant tone of the charter, they cried out that this was nothing but mockery of themselves, that all men capable of drafting so insulting a document should be beheaded, including all lawyers and all those in the Tower. They told the knights very firmly that if the king did not grant them immediately a proper interview then they would storm the Tower and put the king to death, as well as the other traitors. At this threat, which must have alarmed them beyond measure, for the king was the one constant factor, the King's Council surrendered. The first move had failed. It was necessary to put into effect the second part of the Salisbury plan. Word was swiftly sent out to the City wards demanding that all persons between the ages of fifteen and sixty should assemble at Mile End at twelve noon the next day to meet the king in person.

CHAPTER EIGHT

# MILE END

ON FRIDAY, JUNE 14, at seven in the morning, the king left the Tower for Mile End, then a village surrounded by meadows and used by the Londoners during their festivities. Some historians have speculated why the King's Council selected Mile End for the long-delayed conference. One of the motives suggested is that it was an attempt to get the rebel army out of the city, in order to close the gates against the rebels. This reason cannot be seriously considered since it would have meant that the king and the entire court would have been left in the hands of the rebels. Another authority suggests that the reason for choosing Mile End was to draw the army away from the Tower so that Sudbury and Hales might have a chance to escape. A third chronicler, however, bluntly states tnat these two men were deliberately abandoned, so that the lives of the king and the rest of the court might be safeguarded from the wrath of the people.

It was felt that once the rebels had executed the two chief malefactors, their anger would be appeased. Since the anger of the people was directed mainly against these two men, it is probable that this reason is the most likely one. Earlier that morning Sudbury had tried to escape from the Tower by boat, but the attempt was prevented by a sharp-eyed woman who immediately raised the alarm, and Sudbury returned to the Tower.

The ride of the king to Mile End has been used as a convenient stock on which to graft the legend of the heroic boy king, facing the dangerous mob; but according to one of the most reliable accounts (the *Anonimale Chronicle*):

> "The king rode timidly to the place of meeting like a lamb among wolves seemed he, as one in great dread of his life, and he meekly entreated the people standing about."

Accompanying the terrified king were his mother and the entire court, no less terrified. All were there, except the two scape-goats, deserted to save the lives of the rest.

It was a fearful ride to Mile End. All along the route dense crowds of Londoners and others were shouting their demands, and giving full vent to their grievances. So fierce were the threats, so great was the intimidation of the enraged multitude, that the nerves of two of the king's escort failed and, taking advantage of a thinning in the crowd, the Earl of Kent and Sir Thomas Holland, the king's half-brothers, bolted across the fields of Whitechapel.

Almost every few yards, the king was stopped by hands pulling at his horse's bridle. Once he was halted by Thomas Farringdon, who, on his way back from leading Jack Straw to Hales' mansion in Highbury, demanded, "Give me justice on that false traitor, Hales", and the king replied that he "should have all that was just".

This was interpreted by Farringdon as meaning that he could proceed with his work, and he left the throng to join the rebels who had stayed behind to maintain their siege of the Tower. Farringdon made no attempt to enter the Tower. He and the rest of the men waited until instruction came from the Mile End conference, while, inside the Tower, 600 men-at-arms maintained watch.

As the cavalcade entered Mile End fields, the rebel forces were waiting deployed in battle order, with their two standards of St. George again to the fore. As Richard rode forward to the appointed place, the entire army fell upon its knees and welcomed their Lord, King Richard.

A body of rebels headed by Tyler then marched forward and made two requests. The first was that the rebels be allowed to seize all traitors to the king throughout the country and to execute them. The second request was that the king should grant the petitions which they would present to him, and which had already been drawn up in writing.[1]

When Tyler had finished speaking, the king asked to see the petitions. When they were handed to him and read, he, mindful of the careful advice given him by Salisbury, conceded everything. The king then ordered thirty clerks immediately to draw up the charters granting the petitions. He also promised to give his protection to all those counties which desired it. Then, handing over his banner to the rebel leaders so that all might know that they were now acting on his behalf, the king requested that the people should return to their homes.

The first part of Salisbury's plan had been put through. There was no doubt that the peasants were overjoyed. They had won. Their simplicity had been successfully weighed and estimated by the King's Council, and their confidence in the king judiciously exploited. But now the hidden kernel of the scheme, the real reason why all their demands had been so quickly granted, was to be put to the test. Would they go home?

To the peasants it appeared that their objects had been achieved. Nothing could be clearer than the charters which had been granted by the king and which were now being placed in their hands.

> "Know that of our special grace we have manumitted all our liege and singular subjects and others of the county of Hertford, freed each and all of their old bondage, and made them quit by these presents; pardoned them all felonies, treasons, transgressions, and extortions committed by any and all of them, and assure them of our 'summa pax'."

[1] According to Adam of Usk, Tyler also demanded the liberation of all prisoners.

Thus read the charter granted to the men of Hertford, as reported by the St. Albans chronicler, Walsingham, and doubtless all the charters were drawn up in the same way. Judging from the wording of this charter, the demands drawn up in Farringdon's house had been granted in their entirety. All trace has been lost of most of these demands, for most did not require formal revocation by Parliament as did the petitions which had to come before it. The economic concessions had to be formally withdrawn after the suppression of the rising, but the rest of the demands did not require that formality. There can be no doubt that the king also approved the repeal of the Statute of Labourers. This Statute had been fought from the time of ratification, and it is difficult to believe that, having brought the ruling class to a point where they were, at least on the face of it, forced to surrender supreme economic power, the rebels would not have demanded the repeal of this detested Statute. The very phrasing of one of the demands shows that they were determined to abolish the Statute. It states that from henceforth no man shall serve another but of his own free will and for wages, by mutual agreement. This in effect meant the annulment of the Statute of Labourers.

The way in which the king granted the demands should have made even the most simple of the rebels suspicious. Without any show of hesitation or demur the king had agreed to make them the legal government. He had acknowledged that he had been badly advised and led, and that he would from now on recognise only the Commons as his true advisers. It meant that Parliament was no longer to be summoned, since the king had agreed to be guided only by the advice of the people, as represented by Ball, Tyler and others. The acceptance of the demands by the king meant that the power of the overlords was ended, since their incomes had practically been abolished by fixing the rent of land at 4d. per acre. All this had been conceded to the rebels without a murmur of protest by the king and without any attempt at bargaining.

Furthermore, the king had conceded to the rebels the absolute right to proceed against all those whom they regarded as traitors. According to Riley's *Memorials of London* the king said:

> "that they might take those who were traitors against him and slay them wheresoever they might be found."

By now the king and the court had a pretty shrewd idea of whom the rebel forces regarded as traitors. Certainly they had been vocal about their views. The traitors had been attacked openly by John Ball and others who thought like him and their names had been mentioned in some of the earlier Statutes as men against whom slanders were being spread. The desertion of Sudbury and Hales by the Court can now be seen in its true perspective.

Once the rebels had received authority from the king to execute all traitors they were acting, as they thought, in their right as the only legal force in the land. They considered themselves to be no longer rebels. According to tradition, however, the king was considered to be bound by custom, by Parliament and by the council of his natural advisers. Judging by the acts, words and deeds of the rebels after the Mile End conference, it is obvious that the rebel leaders ignored this constitutional custom and considered themselves as the law. It would, however, be true to say that a number of them had some idea of how little the king's apparent concessions, grants, and charters were really worth, otherwise Salisbury's plan would have achieved complete success at Mile End.

Whilst the clerks were copying the charters to be distributed to the various groups of peasants, Wat Tyler was consulting with different bands of rebels. He conferred with Grindcobbe and his men from St. Albans, giving him his opinion on the course of action which should be followed in that town. He authorised Grindcobbe to use the name of the king in all his work in the future. Once these matters had been disposed of, Tyler, together with the body of rebels, rode swiftly to the Tower, scarcely two miles away from Mile End. On his arrival, armed with the king's authority, he had no difficulty in entering. Indeed his entry into this stronghold, held by 600 well-armed men, was carried out in a most friendly way. According to reports the rebels treated the men-at-arms with great friendliness, assuring them that Tyler held no animosity against them, but had come to arrest traitors. If this is correct, then it is obvious that the plan proposed by Walworth would have miscarried, for it is doubtful if the men-at-arms would have obeyed his orders to attack the rebels.

The traitors were soon found. From the moment they had been deserted by the court, Sudbury and Hales had retired to the chapel where they prepared themselves for death. Faced with his judges, the Archbishop made a courageous stand. Before his execution he made a long speech to the rebels, in which he stated that if he were put to death, then the land would be under interdiction, and it says much for the strength of mind of the rebels in this religious age that this most grave threat was received with uproarious laughter. They retorted that they were afraid neither of the Pope nor of the threat of interdiction. Thereupon the Archbishop forgave his executioners and placed his head on the block. After he was beheaded, Robert Hales, John Legge, and Appledore, the king's confessor, were hurried to the block. It is said that the rebels also found the adviser to John of Gaunt, a friar, in the Tower, and that he too was killed.

It is necessary to stress that these men were not murdered. They were executed as traitors by the king's authority on

Tower Hill, the traditional place for executing traitors. The condemned men were at least granted the privilege of a speedy death, without the added refinements of drawing and quartering, so beloved by the king's justices.

After the execution, the heads of the traitors were paraded round the streets in triumph and then put up on London Bridge, where it was customary to expose the heads of traitors and other enemies of the king.

With the Tower in their hands and the traitors it had sheltered executed, the main body of the rebels left the vicinity of the Tower and went to the centre of the city, for there were many still to be punished for their misdeeds. A tribunal was set up before which were brought the enemies of the people. Particularly active in this respect was Thomas Farringdon. It appears from the indictment which was drawn up against him after the revolt had been crushed that he had been given the lists of those condemned to death. Alderman John Horn was engaged in a similar task, but he was concerned with smaller civil offences which did not carry the death penalty. He patrolled the London streets asking whether "any wished to complain to him of any injury", promising "that he and his followers would quickly give them justice". There is a note to the effect that he forced one Robert Morton to pay a fine of £10 to John Pecke, a fishmonger.

In the meantime, the King, who had by now learned of the fate of his erstwhile advisors and of the occupation of the Tower, was escorted to the Royal Wardrobe, in Carter Lane, near Ludgate Hill. The Wardrobe was, apart from the Tower, the most strongly fortified building in London. Here he and his mother established their court, and it was in this building that the Salisbury plan, which was to have the most serious consequences for the victorious rebels, was further elaborated.

When the king and his court left Mile End, the effects of Salisbury's plan quickly began to make themselves felt. The ranks began to divide. Large numbers of exulting rebels began to leave for their villages. To the less determined peasant, who was chiefly concerned with his economic wrongs and not much else, it appeared that the rising had succeeded. The king had pledged his word and had sealed it with his charter and banner of authority. Armed with these, many peasants started to leave for the towns and villages in order to start life anew as freemen.

The division in the rebel forces was not a geographical one. It was not that the men of Essex returned to their homes and the men of Kent remained. It was mainly a question of what might be termed greater or lesser awareness and understanding among the rebels. Those who remained were still unsatisfied and were determined to stay until they had secured the further political and economic changes contained in the demands presented at Mile End. They were not to be fobbed off with a piece of parchment and a banner. They wanted something more real and lasting. Whatever it was, a large number of men remained in London, mainly from Kent, Essex and London, where John Ball had the greatest influence. It was this body of men which caused a great part of Salisbury's plan to miscarry. He believed that with the granting of the charters all would depart, and punitive action could be easily carried out. The strength of the remaining rebel forces was a complication which had not been foreseen, and the next steps to be carried out by the King's Council had to be carefully reviewed.

Following the executions in the Tower, two more leading members of the ruling caste were also executed. It is said that Wat Tyler himself apprehended Richard Lyons, the greatest speculator of them all. This time neither his gold, his powerful protectors, nor Alice Perrers, the late king's mistress, could save him, and he was dragged to the block with as much ceremony as he had earlier shown to people whom he had robbed. The other well-merited execution was that of Richard Imworth, chief jailor of Marshalsea prison. Imworth was notorious for his brutal treatment of the prisoners in his charge, to whom he showed no mercy. "He was a tormentor without pity", wrote the author of the *Anonimale Chronicle*, and for a contemporary writer to have commented on the treatment of prisoners in those days of brutalities must have meant that Imworth was an exceptionally cruel and vicious man.

When the rebels had stormed Marshalsea prison on the Wednesday, Imworth had managed to flee to Westminster where he had sought sanctuary at the shrine of Edward the Confessor. As soon as news of his whereabouts had been received, a body of Kentish men, led by a priest, entered the shrine and captured him. This invasion of the Abbey and the violation of the right of sanctuary, the jeering at the Pope, the laughter at the threat of interdiction at the Tower, all show into what contempt the Church and its traditions had fallen in the eyes of the people. Imworth, too, was dragged to the block in Cheapside and beheaded with scant ceremony.

Much has been written about the attack on the Flemings who had settled in London. Doubtless in this rebellion, as in every major upheaval, acts of injustice were committed by the enraged rebels. But how can the isolated excesses of overwrought peasants and artisans in the early days of a rising be compared with the deliberate and cold-blooded outrages inflicted on the people by the ruling class over years? What of the Statute of Labourers? The outlawing, branding and tortures?

There was a long-standing economic feud between the Londoners and the Fleming weavers, since they had been introduced into London by the drapers and used by them. The

Flemings had also refused to join the London gilds, but had set up their own. The London weavers had carried on a struggle against them for years. It is not surprising, therefore, that advantage was taken of the ferment in London to organise an attack on the Flemings by certain interested parties. The rebels were, after all, after much bigger game than a group of Flemings who were in no way connected with the Statute of Labourers, the Poll Tax, or any other repressive measure. Judging by the fact that the Italian bankers, the Lombards, were also attacked, it appears that other merchant traders, too, utilised the rising in order to dispose of their trade rivals.

Most of Friday and Saturday was occupied in smoking out and cleansing London of the people's enemies. Yet in the midst of this conflict of weeding out and uprooting, the real lair from which the most dangerous of the people's enemies should have been smoked remained untouched. Carter Lane was unmolested and unwatched. The blind spot in all their thinking made this possible. Under cover of this fatal blindness, the King's Council took those further steps which were to lead to the defeat of the rising of 1381.

CHAPTER NINE

# THE RISING IN THE COUNTIES

As soon as the king had granted his false charters to the rebels and had given his authority to the rebel leaders, many set out to spread the news and to rouse the countryside. Men claiming membership of a "Great Society" appear in Cambridgeshire, Norfolk, Suffolk and Huntingdonshire. These, together with local men, some of whom like Wrawe and Grindcobbe had already conferred with Wat Tyler at Mile End, led the rebels against their masters.

Sporadic risings occurred only in the North, the Midlands and in the West, due to the unevenness of the economic and social development in England. In many places the peasants rebelled as soon as the news of the happenings in London reached them. It was a general bid for freedom and in most cases the action taken by the peasants was the same. Records and rolls were destroyed, manors burned, and local oppressors executed. In most areas the rebels were satisfied once they had accomplished this. The peasants generally confined their rising to their own districts and there was little, if any, attempt to link up with other districts and to co-ordinate their activities. The unco-ordinated and sporadic nature of the rising, outside some counties, was obvious, for in the most outlying parts of England risings took place after the rebellion had already been crushed in London.

In East Anglia, however, the rising took on the same shape as in Kent, Essex and London. It was in these counties and in some of the towns that the views of John Ball had most deeply penetrated the people. These counties were by far the most advanced, both politically and economically. The peasantry and labourers in East Anglia felt no less strongly about their grievances than the men of Kent, and were equally prepared to fight for their freedom.

Many anomalies existed in East Anglia. Side by side with the free towns could be found towns whose development was still held in check by the church. Side by side with the freed serf and the free labourer was the tied serf and the restricted artisan, whose manumission was refused by the church or a great lord.

In many cases the church obstinately refused to grant charters to towns under its control, not only because the church was determined to resist all new ideas, but in order to obtain its full legal dues. By maintaining firmly its grip on the economic life of the towns, the church prevented their expansion, retarded trading and manufacture, and treated the burgesses as though they were still villeins. Towns like Bury St. Edmunds and St. Albans were hot-beds of revolt, and the fighting was most violent and bitter there. Here the church was forced to grant charters to the burgesses and rebels, renouncing all manner of rights, dues and tolls, some of which were illegally levied by means of forged documents in the hands of the church authorities. The church was forced to grant freedom to those from whom it had been for so long withheld.

Since so many social groups were affected in the counties, it is natural that representatives of these interests should be found in the leadership and in the ranks of the rebel forces. Men who were leaders in different counties included, for instance, John Wrawe, priest of Suffolk; Sir Roger Bacon, a gentleman and landowner in Norfolk; a number of tradesmen and merchants; and, finally, two outstanding men, William Grindcobbe of Hertfordshire, who had been brought up in a monastic school, and Geoffrey Litster of Norfolk, a dyer.

It will be remembered that William Grindcobbe and some

of his followers in St. Albans had, as soon as they received news of the rising and of the entry into London, hurriedly departed in order to confer with Wat Tyler. On Friday, June 14, they reached Highbury and met the band of rebels led by Jack Straw and Farringdon, engaged in the task of destroying the mansion of Robert Hales. The two groups of men greeted each other with emotion, swore an oath to be true to their cause, and parted shouting their slogan: "For King Richard and the True Commons."

On reaching Mile End, Grindcobbe left some of his men to collect their charters, which were being issued by the clerks, and hurried over to Tyler, with whom he discussed the situation in St. Albans. Tyler gave Grindcobbe his full sppport and said that if the opposing forces proved too strong for the rebels he would "come with 20,000 men to shave the monks' beards", for it was the Abbot of St. Albans who was the mainstay of reaction in the town.

For many years a feud had existed between the Abbey and the town. A charter had been granted to the burgesses of the town by King Offa, claimed the townsfolk,[1] but this Charter had been stolen and hidden by the monks of the Abbey, and now this important market town was completely dominated by the Abbot. Other towns might have their charters of incorporation and their own municipal government, but not St. Albans. Other merchants might have freedom to buy and sell, but not those of St. Albans.

Many towns in the twelfth century had acquired privileges greater than those of St. Albans in the fourteenth century. The monks would not yield an inch.

The burgesses had risen in arms on three occasions, but had been defeated each time. They had gone to law to challenge the rights of the Abbot, but justice was the justice of feudalism, designed to perpetuate the feudal landowners in

[1] There had never been a Charter from King Offa.

their holdings and their privileges, to reinforce their feudal rights, and to maintain their rule. As a consequence judgment was always given in favour of the Abbot. One of the most bitter struggles had raged round the rights of the townsfolk to grind their own corn, but the law gave the verdict to the Abbot, who thereupon confiscated all the millstones in the town and paved his dining-hall with them.

Grindcobbe had long been in the forefront of the struggle against the clergy. He had been excommunicated and imprisoned for his denunciations of the monks, but, as with John Ball, the sentence did not deflect him from his purpose. He was recognised as the leader of the people in St. Albans.

Following his meeting with Tyler, Grindcobbe immediately returned to St. Albans, leaving behind some of his men to complete whatever business remained to be done. That day Grindcobbe travelled thirty miles without taking rest. Upon his return he called together the people of St. Albans and told them of the Mile End meeting with the king, and informed them that the king had granted the rebels full powers to proceed against the Abbot. On hearing this the people immediately marched to the Abbey and destroyed the heavy gates guarding the entrance to the Abbot's park.

The next day they returned, and took full revenge for all the indignities which had been inflicted on them. They drained the fishpond, killed the game, destroyed hedges, raided the preserves and removed all the symbols of privilege which the Abbot had flaunted before them for many a year. Under Grindcobbe's direction, the people dug up their millstones and reclaimed them. At the same time, land which had been illegally enclosed was once again restored as common land. The Abbot's jail was thrown open and the prisoners retried before a court set up by the townsfolk, which released most of them. One prisoner, however, was retried and hanged. Then, with the arrival of the men from Mile

End with the charter, a meeting was arranged between Abbot de la Mare and the rebels.

The hard-faced old reactionary fought long and bitterly but, upon being confronted with the king's charter, he had nothing further to say and surrendered to the people.[1] The charters which recorded the rights of the Abbey were buried in the market place, and the Abbot was made to draw up and seal a new charter, granting the town its freedom.

After the granting of the charter to the town, the townsfolk and the serfs presented their petition. The Abbot conceded to them exemptions from tolls and dues, rights of pasturage on the waste lands of the Abbot, leave to hunt and fish in his woods and ponds, abolition of the monopoly of the seignorial mill, and the right to elect a municipal government to govern the town without interference from the Abbot. Not only was this charter given to the burgesses of St. Albans, but similar charters were also granted to the men of Watford, Barnet and Rickmansworth who had come to the assistance of St. Albans. Indeed the men of St. Albans claimed that they were allied with thirty-two other villages which would come to their aid were this necessary. This in itself was one of the very remarkable happenings which took place during the period of the rising in St. Albans and shows how the Abbot's repression had affected the people.

The petitions were presented to the Abbot after the rebellion had been crushed in London and, although the news reached St. Albans, it did not deter the townsfolk. They had the king's charter, they had his word that the rising was legal, and that was enough.

[1] The use of the king's authority had the desired effect, most opposition being overcome by it. This confirms the belief that the rebel leaders, like the King's Council, used the king's authority for their political ends. It should also be noted that the news had already reached the Abbot of the fate of the Archbishop of Canterbury and the others, and it is possible that this, too, affected his decision, particularly as the rebel who was negotiating with the Abbot pointed out the strength of the commons and Wat Tyler's threat if the demands were not conceded.

Similar risings occurred in Norfolk, Suffolk and Cambridgeshire, and here John Wrawe of Sudbury took charge. John Wrawe was present at the meeting in London before the main body of rebels had entered and returned to Sudbury, giving the signal to rise on Wednesday, June 13. The rebels, under Wrawe, gathered together at Liston, whence they set out on the attack. Here again it is noticeable how similar were the actions of these rebels to those led by Ball and Tyler. Again manor houses were ransacked and burnt together with the rolls, and nothing was done to affect the lives or property of the innocent. During a halt for food, for example, at an inn in Milford Green, the rebels paid for all the food they had consumed (3s. 4d. worth in all). One of the first houses to be destroyed was a manor belonging to Richard Lyons, who had been executed in London. An attack was made on the house of John de Cavendish, Chief Justice of the King's Bench and Justice for the administration of the Statute of Labourers in Suffolk and Essex. He had been awarded an extra salary for acting in this capacity, and his unpopularity was such that all his manors were burnt to the ground.

The rebels marched to Bury St. Edmunds, the history of which was very similar to that of St. Albans. Four previous risings of the townspeople against the clergy had taken place in Bury St. Edmunds, in 1264, 1290, 1304 and 1327. The rebel forces were made as welcome as those who entered Canterbury and London. The Abbey was stormed and, after a search, the Prior was arrested, tried and sentenced to death by John Wrawe. John de Cavendish met a similar fate. He had managed to evade the rebels when his manor was attacked, but Wrawe had sent out a search party, as he did not intend to allow Cavendish to slip through his fingers.

Cavendish was captured in circumstances which showed how intense was the hatred of the people towards such as he. Seeing his pursuers gain on him, he made for the river

Brandon, and, as he was nearing the ferry boat, one Katherine Gamen recognised him and pushed the boat into midstream. Cavendish was beheaded on the spot and his head carried back to Bury St. Edmunds, where it was placed in the pillory, together with the head of the Prior.

Having acted with the king's authority in beheading the traitors, Wrawe turned his attention to the monks. As at St. Albans, they were forced to draw up a charter by which they surrendered all their rights and privileges over the town. This charter, with the deed and muniments of the holdings of the abbey, was presented to the burgesses. Furthermore, in order that the monks should be bound to carry out their part of the charter, they were made to surrender to the town the jewels and holy relics in their possession, as a pledge for their future good behaviour.

Wrawe controlled this area for eight days. According to his indictment Wrawe (who later turned informer) and some of the other rebels were accused of lining their pockets, but here, as with the burning of the Savoy, the petty thefts must be set against the vast amount of wealth which the rebels handled and which was destroyed, untouched.

Despite his subsequent behaviour, Wrawe, whilst he was with the rebels, acted very much in the spirit of the other rebel leaders. He even sent some of his assistants to other areas to give help. Men like Tavell and John Michel were sent to Cambridgeshire. Tavell had been with Wrawe in Bury St. Edmunds and, after the town had been given to the people, he was sent to Ely, where he was awaited. That his visit was expected can be seen by an incident which took place at a bridge. This bridge had been captured by William Combe and was held open until Tavell and his troop of men had ridden through, after which no one was allowed to pass.

Both Tavell and Michel assumed the leadership of the rebel forces on their arrival. On Sunday, June 16, an announcement was made from the pulpit in the monastery that proceedings would be taken against all traitors in the name of the king. The next day the jail was stormed and the prisoners released. Edmund de Walsingham, Justice of the Peace, was tried and sentenced to death. Acting with Tavell and Michel were Geoffrey Cobbe, a man of considerable wealth, Robert Plumer and Richard de Leyster, all of whom played a significant part in the revolt in the surrounding countryside.

Also playing a leading part were Thomas Wroo and Adam Clymme. Wroo was afterwards charged with the offence of agitating the people for a period of six days before and after June 13. He spent his time, says the indictment, urging and instructing the people to join the revolt. The indictment adds that he stated that he was acting in the name of the king. Adam Clymme was indicted for a similar offence. He, too, rode through the county calling on men to rise and commanding that all men, of whatever condition, should immediately cease any service to their lords "except as he (Adam Clymme) might inform them on behalf of the Great Society". Clymme also told the people that they were to execute all those connected with the law, and organised the destruction of rolls and documents.

Further evidence against two other messengers from London exists. One, John Greyston, left Cambridgeshire at the beginning of the rising in the south and remained in London, fighting with the men of Essex and Kent. Later he reappeared at Bottisham, his birthplace, and became the leader of the rising there. Not being in possession of a charter issued at Mile End, he exhibited a legal document which he had in his possession, and said that this gave him full authority to act in the name of the king. The other, John Stamford, though born in Cambridgeshire, was working in London as a saddler. He, too, returned to his birthplace and urged all, in the name of the king, to destroy the traitors.

All these men were acting in conjunction with Wrawe and they accepted his leadership without question; the influence and power which Wrawe exerted over a wide area was similar to that of Wat Tyler.

In Cambridge the Mayor himself led the attack on the university and for three days he and his men were in control. An earlier rising in April had been suppressed, but this time a great deal was achieved. St. Mary's Church was attacked and its valuable stock of charters burned in the market square. The university authorities were forced to surrender their privileges, and made to promise that in the future they would submit to the ruling and the control of the municipal authority.

A prior who had enclosed the common pasturage was made to sign a document, binding himself in the sum of £2,000 not to prosecute the townsfolk for their actions against him. It is interesting to note the caution of the townsfolk during this time. If they were the power in the land, who would take heed of proceedings taken against them by the dispossessed churchmen? Which body was going to condemn the legal and lawful actions of the people? It was precisely because the people could only think in terms of their own town that they took such precautions to protect themselves against any future action.

In another part of Norfolk, Geoffrey Litster, with Sir Roger Bacon as second-in-command, was also taking action. Litster, like Tyler and Grindcobbe, was able to win the regard of the men he led. He appears to have been completely unknown to the authorities before the rising, but very well known to the peasants who made him their leader as soon as the rising began. Litster controlled an area stretching from Cromer to Diss and Yarmouth and, within this wealthy and highly populated district, he firmly established his authority. He carried out the usual attacks on manor houses, burned the rolls and other records and also attacked the foreign merchants and manufacturers who, by the employment of cheap labour and the refusal to observe local custom, had earned the hostility of the native labourers and merchants. Litster's methods were very similar to those of Tyler and Wrawe.

About a week before the rising, Litster had sent out men to ride round the countryside warning all the groups to hold themselves in readiness. The order was obeyed and on June 14 messengers were again sent out calling upon all to march to Mousehold Heath, near Norwich, a traditional meeting place for rebels from time immemorial. The proclamations were made in the name of Litster.

By June 17 most of the rebels had gathered on Mousehold Heath, but, before he gave the order to advance on Norwich, Litster negotiated with Sir Robert Salle, who had been appointed by the local ruling clique to defend the city against the rebels. According to Froissart, Salle was the son of a stonemason and had won fame and wealth in the French wars. He was knighted by Edward III for bravery in the field. In Froissart's account Litster appealed to Sir Robert to join the rebel forces:

> "Robert," said Litster, "you are a knight, and a man of great weight in the country; renowned for your valour; yet notwithstanding all this, we know who you are; you are not a gentleman but the son of a poor mason, such as ourselves. Come with us."

But Salle turned a deaf ear to this appeal, for it was not tactful of Litster to have reminded him of his lowly past. He answered in such a manner that tempers were roused on both sides and, after a brief fight, he was killed.

Norwich was an important city in the Middle Ages, a big trading and manufacturing centre with a large population. Nevertheless it surrendered to the rebels as easily as London. Before their arrival the municipal authorities, alarmed at the fate of Sir Robert Salle, ordered the gates to be closed.

Closed they were, but not for long. As the forces approached the city, the labourers grew so threatening that the burgesses reversed their decision and the rebels were admitted to the city. Various houses were burned by the rebels on entering Norwich, and some of the leading malefactors were tried and beheaded, including those who were responsible for the administration of the Statute of Labourers.

Establishing his headquarters in the city, Litster sent out bands of men to round up the traitors, whilst Sir Roger Bacon was entrusted with the difficult task of subduing Yarmouth, also an important town and one which was regarded with disfavour by the rest of the countryside. According to one of its charters, Yarmouth alone had the privilege of buying and selling, and everyone living in an area within seven miles of the town had to buy and sell their produce in Yarmouth. The members of the gild were so disliked that the poorer merchants, both inside and outside Yarmouth, had protested to Parliament against their extortions. Nevertheless Yarmouth welcomed Sir Roger Bacon, who demanded the charter from the burgesses and, when it was given to him, tore it in half and sent one half to Litster and the other half to Wrawe.[1]

Here, too, several Flemings were beheaded, but this did not prevent the Fleming, Richard Resch, being chosen as the rebel leader in Lowestoft. Bacon also took over the customs and, after appointing his own men as officers, took some of the revenue as funds for the rebel forces, for Litster had opened a central fund in Norwich.

During the brief time he was in power, Litster set up a

[1] The destruction of the charter may have had more than local significance. There was great economic rivalry between London and Yarmouth over the herring trade, since the Yarmouth merchants prevented the London Fishmongers Gild from holding a complete monopoly. It should be recalled that there was a very close contact between the rebels and members of the Fishmongers Gild in London. There was also another charter in existence which gave Yarmouth a right to take tolls and to interfere with traffic to Lowestoft.

tribunal to deal with cases which had arisen before and during the rising. He also sent a petition to the king, asking for charters granting to his district the concessions which had already been granted to the forces at Mile End. He also asked for special treatment for his district. The deputation carrying the petition consisted of three knights and three men of "ignoble" birth.

And so the rising grew and spread. In Bridgwater, Somerset, Nicholas Frampton, a priest, and Thomas Engilby, led the revolt. Frampton had been in London and had witnessed the execution of Sudbury and Hales. He had hastened back to Bridgwater and on June 19 led an attack on the Knights of St. John, old enemies of the town. The rebels destroyed records of the debts owed to the Knights Hospitallers and forced the master to sign a document binding him to pay the town £200. The rising then took the usual course, though when on June 21 news came that the rising had been crushed in London, Engilby fled.

Attacks on the Knights of St. John also took place in Lincoln. Here, too, a priest named William Swepston led the rebels, who were mostly men from Dunsby and from other estates belonging to the Knights Hospitallers. It should be remembered in connection with these widespread attacks that the master of the order of the Knights of St. John was none other than Robert Hales, and it can be assumed that this was the main reason for the attacks.

So the rising ran its course. In many parts of the country the people were impelled as one man by the desire to free themselves from the feudal shackles. But it was not destined to be achieved then, nor in the generations which followed; only for a few brief and glorious days the common folk knew freedom such as they had long dreamed. However, it was not to be enjoyed, for freedom was soon to give way to the reign of the gibbet, the rope and the disembowelling knife.

Soon the masters were to inflict their bloody revenge on a free people. The feudal lords were to impose their justice on the rejoicing peasants.

CHAPTER TEN

# MURDER IN SMITHFIELD

From its retreat in Carter Lane, the King's Council issued a proclamation demanding that now their requests had been granted the rebels were to leave London and return to their villages. The proclamation was ignored, for after Mile End the King's Council had no authority. Yet, despite this, no attempt was made either by John Ball or Wat Tyler or any other of the leaders to arrest the King's Council. The rebels were content to allow Richard to live in the midst of, and be advised by, his Council.

The king's advisors were quick to seize on this advantage and, left in peace, proceeded to introduce the other part of Salisbury's plan. They feared that the longer they delayed the more difficult would it be to regain power. There is no doubt that they were well informed and that news of the development of the rising in the different counties had been brought to them. They were also probably aware of the fact that bands of peasants from the outlying villages of Chiswick, Hendon, Clapham and Croydon had joined the rebels in the city.

Salisbury and the rest of the king's advisors could not but recognise the fact that they were facing a determined body of men who had confidence in themselves, men who were making demands which had the undoubted support of large sections of the lower classes. It was becoming painfully clear that the early idea, that the rebels could be fobbed off and sent home with false promises until the king's men could be rallied, had been too optimistic. Whilst it could not be denied that the guile shown at Mile End had been partially successful and that all those who only wanted economic betterment had accepted the false documents and promises and had gone home contented, nevertheless the fact remained that there was a body of peasants who now wanted more radical reforms, and that these could only be defeated by a bold stratagem.

For some days now Wat Tyler had been pressing for a further interview with the king. He wanted the king's consent to proposals which Tyler himself could easily have put into effect, but this he could not realise. From the beginning the king's advisers had based their hopes on the rebels' respect for the king's person (which they, accustomed to making and breaking kings, did not in the least share) and their dependence on him. It was Tyler's demand for a further interview which, as at Mile End, gave them another opportunity to try to win back all that which was now so gravely threatened.[1]

The further implementation of Salisbury's plan, which was so carefully considered in Carter Lane, could only have been attempted by men who knew that they were in a desperate situation. If they took no action and were content to sit and await events, the chances were that they might remain alive, but possessed of nothing which would make life worth living. If, on the other hand, they took a fighting chance, success would mean certain victory, whilst defeat would only mean certain death which might, in any case, come to them at any moment.

The subsequent events have proved beyond doubt that during Friday and Saturday, June 14 and 15, the group round the king were actively rallying their supporters. One of England's most famous mercenaries, Sir Robert Knolles, was in London with a large body of his men. Neither he nor his property was touched, for the rebels had no score to settle

[1] "Observe how fortunately matters turned out, for had the rebels succeeded in their intentions they would have destroyed the whole nobility of England." (Froissart.)

with him. The King's Council got in touch with him, and with other wealthy merchants and knights in London, many of whom were now prepared to listen to the king's advisers, for the pendulum was beginning to swing the other way.

Apart from burghers like Aldermen Horn and Tonge, the burgesses had become alarmed at the attitude of the rebels. The rising was becoming a threat to them and their not inconsiderable fortunes. It was one thing to use the presence of the rebel peasants to settle scores and to be revenged against a rival gild, or against John of Gaunt and others of the nobility who threatened their rights, but this was another matter. Much valuable property had been destroyed, wealthy merchants killed, whilst law and order had been wrested out of the hands of the authorities and been vested in the hands of peasant hinds, and the lower ranks of the London crafts. They had become the masters of the city. It is possible, too, that demands had been made for the feeding and quartering of the rebel army, which also must have alarmed them, for who was to pay for all this? Enough had happened during the two days the rebels were in control to make a number of the burgesses eager to support any plan which would restore the authority of the king and the King's Council and crush the rebels. At least their lives and their property would be secure and the old way of life, which they understood, restored. Conditions were beginning to ripen for a bold stroke against the rebels. In any case there had been a strong group supporting Walworth from the beginning of the rising.

By Saturday the plan for the counter-attack had been completed, and word was sent to Wat Tyler advising him that the king would grant him an audience in Smithfield at Vespers. After the message had been despatched, the king and his retinue took solemn leave of their women and, for the first time since the rebels had entered London, the queen left the king's side and remained in Carter Lane. The execution of the counter-stroke was dangerous and the women were best out of the way.

Richard and his entire court rode to Westminster, arriving there about three in the afternoon. The agitated and badly shaken monks, not yet recovered from the shock of seeing the rebels tear Imworth from sanctuary, came to meet the king barefoot and carrying the cross. Richard dismounted, kissed the cross and then, followed by the court, knelt in prayer before the shrine and kissed the relics. The prayers were long and fervent and Richard, to whom had been assigned the most dangerous task, confessed and received absolution. Loud and long were the calls to the Almighty for his help in their task; there was the most fervent praying at the shrines, but, despite their prayers, they did not put their complete faith in the Lord. Underneath the silken robes of peace, their official garb, the knights were clad in coats of mail and carried swords, for it was essential, if their plans were to prove successful, that the rebels should not see that they were prepared for battle. And so they set out for Smithfield as the afternoon began to draw in.

Smithfield was, at that time, an open expanse outside the northern walls of London. It was so large that the cattle market was held there every Friday, and the great St. Bartholomew's Fair every year. This fact was important, for the size of Smithfield had been carefully considered by the King's Council when they had decided upon it as the place for the conference with the rebels.

The king and his retinue rode in from Westminster and took up their positions between the Alders Gate and the Lud Gate, right away from the rebel army which was near the London Wall. Confronting them was the entire rebel force, again deployed in battle order, displaying their two great standards and the banners granted by the king at Mile End. It was now no longer an army of tied serfs and labourers. Facing the king was an army of free men who had hewn off their shackles with their own hands, and had flung them into the faces of their old masters, clustered there by the Lud Gate. The common folk were now the masters of England and soon their Wat Tyler would go over to settle matters finally, after which they would be free to return to their homes.

Walworth approached to summon Wat Tyler to meet the king. At Mile End the king had come riding humbly to them, but on that occasion the King's Council were uncertain of the forces they were facing. Today they were firm and decided. On receiving the summons, Wat Tyler, followed by one attendant carrying his banner, rode over to meet the king. Clad in his every-day attire, armed only with a dagger, he rode over to meet an armed and desperate body of men.

He rode to the king, dismounted, dropped on one knee, took the king's hand, shook it vigorously and said heartily: "Brother, be of good cheer and joyful, for you will soon have the fifteenth pledged by the Commons, more than you had before, and we shall be good comrades."[1]

This rough and warm welcome not only expressed Tyler's attitude towards the wretched boy, but showed that probably a plan had been discussed for solving the king's financial problems. The Commons, who had rebelled mainly because of the extortions of their lords, were quite prepared, once the traitors were gone, voluntarily to tax themselves a fifteenth to swell the king's exchequer, thereby solving his immediate financial worries. Did Wat mention this in order to comfort him? It would seem so, for it was obviously a white-faced frightened lad who was facing Tyler, and therefore Wat told the boy the welcome news. But it was a much graver matter than finance which was worrying the king at the moment. It was a far deeper and uglier thing.

[1] There is a good deal of contradiction between the different accounts of the Smithfield meeting. This version is from G. Kriehn's account, but it has been questioned by other writers.

With the greetings over, the king demanded to know the reason why the rebels had not returned to their homes. Tyler, uncowed by this approach, so different from the earlier conference, swore an oath that no one would depart until his further demands had been granted and he added, for the ears of the intently listening retinue, "much the worse will it be for the lords of this realm if this charter be refused".

Richard asked for the details of the charter and in reply Wat Tyler read out a series of radical demands.

> "Let no law but the Law of Winchester prevail, and let no man be made outlaw by the decree of judges and lawyers. No lord shall exercise lordship over the Commons; and since we are oppressed by so vast a horde of bishops and clerks, let there be but one bishop in England. The property and goods of the holy church should be taken and divided according to the needs of the people in each parish, after making provision for the existing clergy and monks, and finally let there be no more villeins in England, but all to be free and of one condition."

So demanded Wat Tyler, in the name of the Commons of England and, when he had finished, the king, as at Mile End, granted all the demands:

> "All that you have asked for I promise readily if only it be consistent with the regality of my crown. And now let the commons return home, since their requests have been granted."

The stripling could scarcely have understood the meaning or the implications of the demands read out by Tyler, but since his instructions were to accept whatever conditions were laid down by the rebels, except "it be consistent" with the retention of his kingship, he carried them out implicitly.

The charter demanded by the rebels can be grouped under three heads: legal, economic and religious.

The demand that no law but the law of Winchester should

prevail was a most important one. The Statute of Winchester had been passed by Edward I in an endeavour to put down growing violence and disorder. Highways to market towns were to be widened, and kept clear for 200 feet on either side of the roadway, the responsibility for this being placed upon the lord of the manor. The Statute further placed upon the people the responsibility for law and order in their areas—mainly upon the freemen, not the tied serfs, for the freemen were entitled to bear arms.

In demanding the repeal of all legislation which had gone against the spirit of the Law of Winchester, the rebels believed that they were demanding the restoration of their ancient civil rights, however unreal that belief was. The Statute of Labourers and the rest of the repressive legislation ratified over some time had meant the gradual transference of their rights into the hands of the growing bureaucracy, into the hands of a growing centralised State. The Statute of Labourers and the other statutes had meant the creation of special bodies of men acting as justices of the peace, poll-tax collectors, etc. The unrest of the people had necessitated the setting up of these punitive bodies in order to enforce the oppressive legislation. With the Law of Winchester in its original form, it would not have been possible to administer the Statute of Labourers. Where would the feudal lords have found the peasant willing to arrest his brother for resisting low wages and enforced labour?

It must be remembered that the feudal state was loosely knit, and that there was a great deal of tightening of the state apparatus during the fourteenth century. Although the serfs had been oppressed, certain traditional rights were maintained. To the rebel it appeared that the Law of Winchester had perpetuated this tribal tradition. It carried the people back, commented Bishop Stubbs in his *Constitutional History,* to ". . . the earliest institution of the race—Watch and

Ward. . . ." The Law of Winchester made full provision for the suppression of lawlessness and crime and, if that were so, there was no necessity for the creation of special bodies of men for the sole purpose of carrying out punitive acts against the common people.

The second demand—the abolition of outlawry—was also directed against the reactionary policy of the feudal rulers and their coercive machinery. Outlawry was one of the harshest sentences imposed on a citizen. It meant the loss of all legal rights, property and protection. Originally the outlaw could legally be killed on sight by anyone. The harsher provisions of this sentence were slowly becoming obsolete. For instance, by 1381 the outlaw could not legally be killed on sight, but operation of the Statute of Labourers not only increased the number of sentences of outlawry but brought into use a new and brutal innovation. So many of the serfs and labourers fled from the administration of the Statute of Labourers that in 1360 an enactment was passed re-stating that all who fled would be outlawed. The fugitive, continued this measure, when caught, was to be returned to the place from whence he had fled, there branded on the forehead with a letter "F" and imprisoned. It was against this that John Ball and his followers had protested so vigorously and thus it had found its place in the demands put before the king at Smithfield.

Of the other demands affecting the economic and religious life of the country, the demand for the total abolition of serfdom had been proposed at Mile End, but it is obvious that the rebels regarded this as so important that they again put the demand in their Smithfield programme, elaborating it to show that they intended that all men should be equally free, that none should be legally dependent on another save the king alone. This was a new factor which, taken together with the freeing of the serf, would have had a shattering effect upon the whole fabric of feudalism in England.

So far as the church was concerned, the demand that the estates of the church should be confiscated was consistent with the policy so often preached by John Ball. No church property was to remain in the hands of the clergy. After provision for their sustenance, and nothing more, had been paid, the remainder of the property was to be placed at the disposal of the people. The church, the greatest expropriator of wealth from the peasants, was to be expropriated. The rebels were not against the priesthood, but they made careful differentiation. As a rule, the poor village priest was a good friend of the people. Usually he was as poor as his parishioners and he had, together with his flock, often put forward a request for higher wages, which was as often refused by the bishop. Since all who worked for a wage came under the jurisdiction of the Statute of Labourers, the village priest was included. It is not surprising, therefore, that apart from other causes some of the leading figures in the rebellion came from the ranks of the poor priests. The rebels were very careful to distinguish between the rich cleric and the parish priest. They declared their willingness to support the poor priest and give him "easy sustenance" compared to the "reasonable sustenance" offered to the rest of the clergy. This "reasonable sustenance", they let it be understood, would only be granted to the more wealthy cleric from the proceeds left after the church property had been distributed amongst the people and their needs satisfied.

The church authorities were the most powerful in England. It has been estimated that they owned one-third of the land.[1] They possessed vast manorial estates which yielded great profits from labour and money rents. They took for themselves the profits of justice in their manors. They owned forests, tolls, market dues, rights of pasturage, mines, fisheries and harbours.

[1] This was a traditional estimate.

This meant that the church was the major economic power. The confiscation of all its property and the annulment of its rights would mean that the entire income of the church would revert to the people, except for that part of it which would go to the provision of no more than a reasonable sustenance to priests and abbeys. (It will be remembered that Ball had stated that priests should not be given tithes and oblations except by those richer than themselves.) It meant that the tenants need no longer pay rents; that the rights of forest and pasture would be free and that all fetters upon trade, such as tolls, market control and all limitations placed on the activities of merchants would be removed. Every serf tied to clerical land would be free, holding his hand directly from the king, in whom would be vested all property rights. This programme for dealing with the temporal income and the possessions, is clearly distinct from the programme for dealing with the spiritual income of the parishes which was to be divided between the parishioners after the incumbent was paid and would be carried out on a parish basis.

The demand for the confiscation of the wealth of the church (finally carried out by Henry VIII) was, of course, not new. Edward I and Edward III had already tasted some of the forbidden fruits by the temporary confiscation of alien priories. Wycliffe, too, had advocated this confiscation. What was an entirely new factor, however, was the rebels' demand that the church lands should revert back to the peasants, from whom the church's wealth had been extorted. It was Wycliffe's intention to parcel out the church's wealth amongst the impoverished gentlemen of the time, who would then proceed to govern the people justly. This did not at first seriously alarm the authorities, but when the rebels demanded with the force of arms that it should be distributed to the poorest in the land, the danger had to be faced.

The rebels wanted drastic church reform. They wanted a

king, divorced from the ruling class, and under their control. They also wanted one bishop who would be as supreme in matters spiritual as would the king in matters temporal. The church hierarchy would be abolished, the monasteries disestablished, and the church's power broken.

It was to this vast programme of reform that the king had bound himself by accepting Wat Tyler's demands. Perhaps some of the gentlemen present realised the extent of the demands and their consequences, for when Tyler had finished and the king had formally accepted the charter, a deep silence fell upon the group. The time for action had arrived. The silence, however, was broken by Tyler. Flushed by the success of his negotiations, overheated and exhausted not only by his speech but by the long weeks of activity, he felt the strain now that it was all over. He longed for a drink, a good wholesome drink of ale, the drink of the commons. He called for water so that he might rinse the dust and dryness from his mouth, and in order that he might better savour the beer. In front of the entire court he rinsed his mouth and spat out the water. Then he drank a great draught of ale, to make the end of the old and to toast the new. Refreshed and contented, he mounted his little horse to ride over to his people and to break the great news, but before he could spur his horse forward he found himself surrounded by the king's retinue. He and his attendant were cut off from the rebel army that stretched almost out of sight in the gathering dusk.

From out of the narrowing, menacing circle a young page, following instructions, called out that he knew this Wat Tyler who was, he said, the greatest thief and robber in the whole of Kent. Wat Tyler grew angry, yet he was prudent even in his anger, and asked that his traducer should come before him, for was he not now the king's chief counsellor? The youth refused to leave the safe shelter of the surrounding circle. Instead he used still more insulting language.

Tyler again demanded that his accuser should stand before him and this time the courtiers themselves brought the youth to the front. The page reiterated his charges. Daintily apologising for arguing in front of the king, he insisted that he was speaking the truth and did not deserve the death which Wat Tyler was now demanding. Until this moment Tyler had given no excuse for the king's party to draw their swords to strike. They drew in still closer, and Tyler drew his dagger, perhaps to strike at the jeering provoking youth, perhaps because he only now realised that he was in the most terrible danger. But this was the one move for which they were waiting. It was for this one action that they had enacted the whole scene. They had staked everything upon this situation and, with the care and skill of professional gamblers, had carefully nursed their victim until the moment most favourable to them had arrived. It was a desperate venture and upon it they had placed the highest stakes: a kingdom and their lives.

Walworth charged forward crying that he would arrest any who drew a weapon in the king's presence. On he came, lusting to avenge the burning of his brothels. Wat Tyler struck back at him with hard blows of his dagger, but his thrusts glanced aside harmlessly on the cuirass hidden beneath his robes. Walworth struck twice, and Wat Tyler fell back on his horse, wounded in the head and neck. Then the whole royal circle ran amok. Well might Ralph Standish and John Cavendish hack and thrust at the man lying upon his horse, stricken almost to death, helpless and unarmed, cut off from the help of his friends, for they were avenging their class for the humiliation suffered at his hands. At the sight of the stricken man their courage, which had oozed away when they had first seen the peasants in action, returned and they struck hard to avenge their shame and to regain their lost property and privileges.

The vigour of Wat's life told. With failing strength he spurred his horse towards his comrades, who were straining their eyes in an effort to see what was amiss, but his horse had only gone four score paces when, succumbing to his wounds, Tyler fell to the ground.

The rebel army was in an uproar. It could see the flashing of steel in the distance, but was too far away to see what was wrong. Then, at the sight of Tyler's horse dashing through the throng of knights, their suspicions were aroused, but, before the arrows could leave their bows, the king was dispatched towards them. Legend has painted a brave boy king making a speech full of courage and daring. This is nothing but the veneer used by the chroniclers to cover a state murder. Richard made no noble speech. It is true that he showed daring in riding forward, but he, too, had been heated by the murder of Tyler, and he had been assured many times that the rebels would not harm him.

He stuttered out a few hasty words. "Tyler has been knighted," he said. "Your demands have been granted." They were all to march to St. John's Fields, where Wat Tyler would be waiting for them. Blindly obeying the king, in whom they still had implicit trust, and whom they still had no reason to doubt, they marched to St. John's Fields of their own accord, for Richard did not lead them. He hastily left by another route with some of his retainers, and was escorted through the city by Walworth. In accordance with the plan, which was being followed to the last letter, his court had ridden at once into London, to mobilise and lead into action the armed groups of king's men, who had been secretly gathering in the various wards throughout the day.

When Wat Tyler had been struck down, the two Aldermen, Walter Sybyle and John Horn, who had watched horrified from a vantage point on the city walls, made a final attempt to save the day. Riding from Aldersgate to Westcheap, they sounded the alarm: "Citizens, shut your gates and put a guard upon the walls, otherwise all is lost."

Another version of their attempt to rally the citizens is that they rode through the city calling on the people to man the walls, stating that the king had been killed and that they should ignore appeals to march to his aid, but in any case it was too late. Although they managed to close the Aldersgate, they could not prevent the gathering of the Lord Mayor's forces to aid the king. Large numbers of armed men answered the call, consisting of mercenaries, retainers of the lords, wealthy merchants and their followers, together with other citizens who had become alarmed at the development of the rising.[1] These forces came pouring out from twenty-four different wards. Led by Sir Robert Knolles, Brembre, Philpot, and others of the king's retinue, they so deployed their forces that by the time the rebel army had reached St. John's Fields and was drawn up awaiting Tyler, the king's forces were able to emerge from the North-West Gate and surround the rebels "like sheep within a pen".

In the meantime, after he had escorted the king through the city to St. John's Fields, the implacable Walworth returned to Smithfield to find Wat Tyler. The plan of Salisbury demanded the death of Tyler, and the Lord Mayor wished to carry out this part of it to the very letter. When he arrived at Smithfield he found Tyler's body gone, and finally learned that he had been carried into St. Bartholomew's Hospital by some of his sorrowing comrades. He lay dying in the master's chamber, but Walworth was not to be deflected by such a trifle. He stamped in and, pulling the dying man from the bed, dragged him along the ground into the middle of Smithfield. There he cut off Tyler's head and, impaling it on his

[1] It is possible that some of these may have been stampeded by the cry raised "they are killing the king," and went to his rescue rather than actually to attack the rebels.

lance rode in triumph to his king.

Upon the arrival of Walworth with the ghastly head of their leader impaled on the lance, the rebels were overcome with horror and alarm. They had expected to see Wat Tyler in the full glory of his newly won honours. Instead they saw his bleeding head on a lance. With cries of dread and fear they sank to their knees amidst the wheat fields, back to the ground from which for a few brief and glorious days they had risen unshackled and free. Leaderless, bewildered and stampeded, their serfdom fell back on their shoulders.

Again the lust to kill overwhelmed the lords and rich burghers. They demanded a massacre, but they were held back by the wiser council of Salisbury and Sir Robert Knolles. Perhaps they understood the courage of despair, which only a brief hour before had actuated them; but above all they realised that they who were now so humbled were also armed, and that in the counties the rising was still gathering momentum. Again Salisbury's council was accepted. It was necessary to proceed quietly, to postpone their revenge for a few more days, when the peasants would be dispersed and all would be ready. Then, and only then, was the time to strike, and to strike hard, with neither mercy nor pity, for they could then strike without the fear of retaliation.

With the acceptance of this wiser council, it was made known to the Commons that, since their demands had been granted, they could now disperse to their homes. Upon this proclamation, the rebels, headed by two knights, allowed themselves to be led through and away from London. Watched by an exulting court, they marched through the wheatfields, heavy with grief at the thought that their beloved Wat Tyler was not with them to share in their triumph.

* * *

The king rode back to his mother. "Ah, fair son," she cried, "what pain and anguish have I had for you this day," to which Richard made reply: "Certes, madam, I know it well. But now rejoice and praise God, for today I have recovered my heritage that was lost, and the realm of England also."

It had been as close as that.

* * *

In view of the general acceptance of the account written by Froissart, it is necessary to analyse carefully the whole course of the proceedings which ended in the murder of Wat Tyler in Smithfield,[1] in order to establish the fact that it was a carefully planned state murder.

The policy of Salisbury adopted at the meeting of the King's Council held on Thursday night in the Tower, was, in effect, to make false promises to the rebels and issue charters to them which were not meant to be fulfilled; after receiving these "concessions" it was believed that the peasants would disperse peacefully to their homes, satisfied. Once they were out of London and scattered among the towns and villages again, the king, backed by a powerful army and fully prepared to meet any trouble, could easily have rescinded the charters, since he would have claimed that they were illegally extorted by force, and not granted by Parliament. The king was in no position, constitutionally, to grant the demands. That was only the prerogative of Parliament. The gesture of granting the charters was merely a trick, deliberately played to deceive the rebels and get them to return to their homes, for the pledged word would not be kept.[2]

The conference at Mile End was a farce enacted to gain time and to divide and confuse the rebels, but it also served another purpose. It enabled the royal party to be absent from

[1] G. Kriehn's version is here fully accepted and utilised.

[2] In referring to the second series of promises made by the king in Smithfield, G. M. Trevelyan, in *England in the Age of Wycliffe*, says that "such promises exposed the rulers to the odious charge of bad faith". He continues: "Such professions may possibly have been the only way of saving the State. Princes have often thought so."

the Tower whilst the scapegoats they had deliberately left behind them were executed. This, too, was part of the deliberate plan to satisfy the demands of the rebels. What did a few lives, false pledges and a handful of fake charters matter when a kingdom was at stake?

Salisbury's policy succeeded in dividing the rebel forces, but only partially, for a large force of rebels remained behind in London. The chief weakness of his plan was his lack of comprehension of the forces he and the rest of the ruling class were facing, of the tremendously deep feeling which had been stirred by the rising, and what it represented.

Disturbed at only the partial success of their plans at Mile End, the King's Council retired to the Wardrobe in Carter Lane to consider their next steps. They kept a firm grip on their trump card, the king. With him under their control, they still had a fighting chance. They were now less in the dark. They had seen how the king had been received by the rebel forces, and they also knew who were their leaders and spokesmen. The King's Council understood the peasantry sufficiently well to know that if they could remove the leaders it would then be easy to get control of the rebel force by carefully exploiting the king's authority, and the rebels' belief in his impartiality. This was the thread used to weave the net which trapped Tyler. They could now more clearly estimate the extent and strength of the opposition they had to face and, consequently, what may be called the second part of the policy elaborated by Salisbury was reformulated and developed with the utmost care and detail, for no word leaked out to the rebels of the counter-moves which were being planned under their very noses. How grimly the situation had changed.

The King's Council utilised the interval between the meeting at Mile End and the conference at Smithfield to perfect their plan. They worked out almost to the last detail all that had to be done. All the actors in the drama to be staged had been briefed and rehearsed before the cavalcade moved off to Westminster to pray for the success of their endeavours. That is why they wept and prayed so fervently, and why the king, to whom had been assigned the most dangerous part, had confessed his sins. He had no desire to leave the earth unshriven.

They had carefully selected the spot in Smithfield where they took up their positions, for they had known which gates were to be manned by their supporters. They took up their positions as closely as possible to these gates so as to enable the men detailed to lead the armed groups of the king's supporters, to enter the city without the slightest delay, for there were large numbers of armed men, organised in twenty-four different wards in the city waiting the order to go into action. Only half an hour elapsed between the murder of Wat Tyler and the arrival of the king's forces at St. John's Fields. Was it possible in so short a space of time to gather together large bodies of armed men from twenty-four wards, to give them instructions, and so deploy them that, at a given signal, they could all emerge in the best tactical manner and surround the rebel forces?

Moreover, we are told that the king spontaneously rode over to the rebel forces. How then did the widely scattered force know that the king had ordered the rebels to march to St. John's Fields? There can be only one explanation. That is, that the waiting groups had been given their general instructions before the Smithfield conference, and that the king's retinue knew what proposals the king was going to make to the rebels and where they would be found. Only when every point had been settled and the plans decided, was the proclamation made granting an audience at Smithfield.

This explains why the great expanse of Smithfield was chosen, and why the meeting was timed for Vespers. By the time the negotiations were well under way, dusk would be setting in and it would be more difficult for the rebel forces to see what was happening in the close circle round Tyler. It was because of this that Wat Tyler was called over to speak to the king, instead of the king with his retinue of 200 armed men riding over to the rebels. Above all it explains the extraordinary behaviour of the young page. Some historians state that Wat Tyler was deliberately rude to the king and wanted to provoke him, but they give no explanation for this peculiar action, except that Tyler was a rude artisan and a rebel. They avoid explanation by stirring up prejudice.

But the policy of the rebels was to obtain the active support and sympathy of the king for their programme. Why, then, should Wat Tyler, who was, as these writers admit, a man of great common sense, suddenly depart from a policy which he had helped to mould and which, up to that very moment, had been so scrupulously carried out? Whenever Wat Tyler occupies the centre of the stage, he appears as an able negotiator. His task was to negotiate a number of concessions and to win a number of demands, and he appears to have done this admirably and successfully, although the concessions granted were trickery. Why, then, should he suddenly behave in a childishly irresponsible manner and try to provoke a dispute with the king, particularly when, apart from his solitary attendant, he was completely alone, and some distance from the main body of his men?

Had he been a malicious man, he could have wiped out the entire court, either at Mile End or in Carter Lane. Who could have stopped him? Was he seized with a sudden desire to show his power? But he had already held power from the moment he had entered London and each succeeding day, with the development of the rising in the country, his power was being strengthened.

There is no logical explanation for this peculiar behaviour

described by the hostile chroniclers. On the other hand, there is every reason to believe that it was in the interests of the King's Council to provoke Wat Tyler, who was so difficult to tackle in any other way, to make him draw his weapon in the king's presence, and thereby cause the pretext for the murder. The page, therefore, was instructed to insult Tyler, in order to try to provoke him. This has been described in the most vivid way by the author of the *Anonimale Chronicle*:

> "During all this time that the king was speaking, no lord or councillor dared or wished to give answer to the commons in any place save the king himself. Presently Wat Tighler, in the presence of the king, sent for a flagon of water to rinse his mouth because of the great heat that he was in, and when it was brought he rinsed his mouth in a very rude and disgusting way before the king's face. And then he made them bring him a jug of beer, and drank a great draught and then, in the presence of the king, climbed on his horse again. At this time, a certain valet from Kent, who was among the king's retinue, asked that the said Walter, the chief of the commons, might be pointed out to him. And when he saw him, he said aloud that he knew him for the greatest thief and robber in all Kent. Watt heard these words and bade him come out to him, wagging his head at him in sign of malice; but the valet refused to approach, for fear that he had of the mob. *But at last the lords made him go out to him, to see what he [Watt] would do before the king. . . .*"[1]

This account makes it clear that Wat Tyler was deliberately insulted and falsely accused, so that his reactions might be used as the pretext to murder him. His death would mean the removal of the most dangerous rebel leader, for it was he who appeared to be keeping the rebel force together. Some of these councillors had been in France during the rising of the French peasants, the Jacquerie, and they had been in close

[1] Author's italics.

touch with the French nobility when Cale, the leader of the French rebels, had been invited to attend a conference with the French nobility to discuss terms with them. It is quite possible that some of the English nobility had been present in the council chamber when Cale was stabbed to death, for there was a truce between the two countries. This had happened in 1358, and was not too far distant in time to have escaped the memory of one like Salisbury, or the others.

Murder was a recognised method of ridding oneself of political rivals and of awkward customers. Edward II had been murdered in a manner almost too brutal to be believed:

> "On 21st September, 1327, Gurney and Mantraver, after the Bishop of Hertford had given the word 'Kill Edward. Never fear, 'tis good', gave Edward a good dinner and a good supper and put on every appearance of kindness. That night they stole into his room with some attendants. . . . They threw a heavy table on the upper part of his body as he lay in bed and, with a red hot spit, perforated and lacerated his entrails through the anus . . . the shrieks bore into the midnight darkness the tidings of as revolting an outrage, as black and savage a murder as ever contrived."[1]

If kings were murdered by such methods, Richard II's advisers would not hesitate to plan the murder of a mere rebel workman.

The murder of Wat Tyler, therefore, was most carefully conceived. Everything went according to plan. The only hitch appears to have been the vitality of Wat Tyler which enabled him to drive his horse through the circle of men who were stabbing and slashing at him with their swords. The distance, however, was too long and his wounds too severe for him to reach his comrades. He fell from his horse before he was close enough for them to see his grievous condition. The writer of the *Chronicle* already quoted is here most explicit:

[1] J. Mackinnon: *The History of Edward III*, p. 15.

". . . and when the commons saw him fall, *and knew not for certain how it was,* they began to bend their bows and to shoot, wherefore the king himself spurred his horse and rode out to them commanding them that all should *come to him*[1] to Clerkenwell Fields."

This careful writer records no heroic speech by the "beautiful boy", as G. M. Trevelyan calls the king. There was only time for a very brief hurried word, one which would have the effect of allaying the immediate suspicion that Wat Tyler had been slain. This, surely, can be the only feasible explanation why the rebel army, which had fought its way to victory, had threatened the king and his nobility with death, had executed traitors and had shown such discipline and restraint in the early days of their entry into London, did not strike back. "They knew not how it was." This is the phrase which explains their hesitation and doubt, and their immediate acceptance of the word of the king, which they had no reason to mistrust. Represented at Smithfield were the most convinced rebels, those most determined to get their way. The weaker and the less understanding had long departed from Mile End to their homes. The majority of these men had most likely marched under Tyler all the way from Maidstone. Would such a body have stood idly by and seen their leader slaughtered without taking the most ruthless and bloody revenge? The evidence goes to show that they could not see what was going on. Otherwise why should they have been so horrified and alarmed when they saw the bleeding head of Tyler on Walworth's lance?

The *Anonimale Chronicle* states it clearly:

"*. . . and when the commons saw that their chieftain Wat Tyler was dead in such a manner* they fell to the ground there amongst the wheat, *like beaten men.*"[2]

[1] The phrase should be noted: It is that they should "come to him" not "follow him". Author's italics.

[2] Author's italics.

Men who had seen their leader murdered without attempting retaliation and had accepted the leadership of the king without a murmur, could not have behaved in this way. To the many historians who regard such risings as sudden outbursts of mob fury, indifference on the part of the rebels towards their leader is quite conceivable. Superficial evidence to support this view can easily be obtained, since the official accounts of the murder were written with a political purpose in view; to bring honour to the king, his court and the feudal nobility, and contempt and hatred for the rebels and their cause. It was in the interests of contemporary writers to flatter the king. They wrote as the representatives of the feudal nobility and the king personified in their eyes the upper strata of feudal society. As for Froissart, no court writer could have written in any other strain. Indeed he openly admits that his account of the rebellion was written "in order that gentlemen and others may take example and learn to correct such wicked rebels", and it is he who is most responsible for the veneer used to cover this state murder. Richard II was presented with a copy of Froissart's history and Richard was one of Froissart's chief patrons.

There remains the sorrowful incident in St. John's Fields, where the rebels fell to pieces and lost their morale. Here the whole circumstances have to be taken into consideration. The king had informed them that all their demands had been granted and their leader, with his new honours, would be awaiting them in St. John's Fields. What, then, must have been their feelings when, after a brief interval, bodies of armed men burst out simultaneously from the north-west gates and surrounded them? Then, following on this, Tyler's head is carried in triumph on Walworth's lance. It had taken nearly thirty years of hard and patient labour by John Ball and others to bring the serfs to the point of rebellion. It had taken years to break down the terrible servility and fear towards their lords. External factors had, of course, made it possible. Historical development had sharpened the struggle but man had still to take up, shape and control the tide of development.[1] It was John Ball, Wat Tyler, and others who helped the serfs in striving to free themselves from bondage. But, despite all the preaching, explanation, and encouragement of John Ball and his companions, at bottom the peasants were the products of their environment, of feudalism. They were ruthlessly exploited, oppressed, ignorant, superstitious, dependent upon strong men, leaders, who would guide them and tell them what to do. They were what feudalism had made them and, when faced with the sudden apparition of death, with the head of their slaughtered leader, with the sight of the king's forces and their overlords, fully armed and in such large numbers, all their old fear and servility rose and submerged them. A wave of terror passed through the ranks, throwing them back on to their knees.

Whilst they were temporarily overcome by panic and fear, however, it was not for long. The king had made promises, had issued his charters, and their fighting spirit again asserted itself when they found that they had been cruelly tricked, that the charters were not even worth the parchment on which their freedom had been recorded. They became determined to fight for what had been pledged them by the king. Soon many of them were dying heroic deaths in action against the king's forces, in defence of their hardly won freedom, and for the maintenance of their just rights.

[1] "The laws of history are blind laws in so far as they are independent of our wills, but they are worked upon by conscious man." (Karl Marx.)

CHAPTER ELEVEN

# THE KING STRIKES BACK

As THE LAST ranks of the rebel army disappeared through the wheatfields, the king called before him Walworth, Brembre and Philpot. These he made knights. Walworth, as Lord Mayor, spoke for them all after the honours had been awarded. He said that he was "not worthy or able to have or to spend a knight's estate, for he was but a merchant and had to live by traffic". And what a traffic that was!

After this ceremony the king handed over control of the city to the newly knighted merchants and Sir Robert Knolles. He gave them full power, and they made good use of it.

Bands of armed mercenaries combed London, murdering and slaying. Scores of rebels were dragged to the block in Cheapside and beheaded. Anyone who looked like a peasant, or was considered to be one, was slain, whilst many of them were handed over to the relatives of the executed Flemings, to take revenge in whichever way they wished. Several of the rebel leaders were captured and killed without the semblance of a trial. John Kerby, Alan Threder and Jack Straw were among those slain that night.

Straw is supposed to have confessed his guilt before his death but, devoid of all the childish comments by the monks who recorded this "confession", it is merely a statement of his views, which mostly coincides with the demands already made by Tyler. Apart from the more absurd phrases interpolated for political motives, such as "they intended to divide all the riches among themselves" and "they intended to set alight to the four corners of London", Straw said that the rebels intended to rid themselves of landlord rule, to establish a democratic church, to abolish the monarchy after the king had become reconciled to the people, and, instead of a parliament, each county was to have self-government. England was to have become a federation of self-governing communes.

With London safely held, the King's Council turned its attention to the revolt in the counties. They sent out an urgent appeal to all the lords in the surrounding country to rally to the king's standard, which he had set up in Blackheath. To Blackheath came flocking all those who wanted revenge and who scented blood and good hunting. From their hide-outs in the woods, from the barricaded manor houses, crept the gentry, their courage restored now that the most dangerous of the rebel forces had been disbanded. By June 18, sufficient troops had gathered together, and the King's Council issued a proclamation ordering, in the king's name, the arrest of all malefactors and dispersal of all unruly gatherings. The force at Blackheath was divided into large companies and each company was assigned an area for pacification. The main force, with the king at its head, rode into Essex for its Roman holiday, for Essex had refused to submit. The rebels of Essex stated that all they had done had been approved by the king—as indeed it had—and their acts were therefore legal. If the king now intended to wrest from them what was rightly theirs, they were prepared to defend their rights to the death.

On June 22, the army rode into Waltham, where the king set up his standard. On his arrival, a deputation from the large rebel force awaited him and boldly demanded the ratification of the charters granted to them by the king. They further demanded all those rights which were theirs now that they were free men.

In reply the king, or rather the King's Council, gave vent to all its pent-up savagery. The "waiting period", suggested by Salisbury, was evidently deemed at an end, and now it was safe to unmask. To the demand of the men of Essex that he keep his pledged word, the King's Council, as Stowe tells us, answered through Richard:

> "O most vile and odious by land and sea, you who are not worthy to live when compared with the lords whom ye have attacked; you should be forthwith punished with vilest deaths were it not for the office ye bear. Go back to your comrades and bear the king's answer. You were and are serfs, and shall remain in bondage, not that of old, but in one infinitely worse, more vile without comparison. For as long as we live, and by God's help rule over this realm, we shall attempt by all our faculties, power and means to make you such an example of offence to the heirs of your servitude as that they may have you before their eyes as in a mirror, and you may supply them with a perpetual ground for cursing and fearing you, and fear to commit the like."

With these sentiments ringing in their ears the messengers were dismissed, and in order to make matters still more clear the King's Council issued a further proclamation, warning the people that in no way did the king sympathise with the cause of the rebels. He did not approve of their doings, nor were the peasants acting according to his instructions.

When the messengers brought the king's reply back to the great body of men gathered at Billericay, they declared that they would either enjoy the freedom which they had won or else die in its defence. They sent for reinforcements, which came from Great Baddow and Rettenden. Then, according to the military tactics of the time, they built a strong defensive position by some woods; guarding their flanks with ditches and carts chained together, and awaited the king's forces.

They had not long to wait. Against this body of poorly armed men, the King's Council despatched a large force of heavily armed cavalry and men-at-arms, the vanguard of the king's forces. The engagement took place on June 28, and after a short sharp battle the palisades were stormed in a cavalry charge. The rebels retreated, leaving 500 dead on the field, but despite the heavy losses, the force remained intact. They retreated to Colchester and Huntingdon where they tried to get the people to join their ranks and make a stand against the king's forces. But the people would not join them and the rebels marched to Sudbury, in an attempt to link up with John Wrawe. To their dismay they found that Wrawe had already been defeated and instead of meeting friends and allies, they had to face fresh troops. There was another fight, but the odds were overwhelming. Many were killed, and others were either stabbed to death while hiding in the thickets, or captured. But a number managed to escape, no one knows whither, except that for some time to come isolated risings took place in various parts of the country. Prior to this, a band of men had marched to Guildford, where they also tried to organise a stand, but without success.

Robert Tressilian, Lord Chief Justice in place of Cavendish, earned an infamous reputation for himself as one of the long line of English judicial butchers. He took full revenge on the rebels. It is said that in the early days of the suppression he spared no one who appeared before him, sentencing so many to death that in some places nine or ten rebels at a time were hanged upon a single beam. When Tressilian and the king arrived at Chelmsford, yet another proclamation was issued, in which the king revoked all the charters he had granted and withdrew all the pledges he had made at Mile End.

By such methods did the nobility steadily destroy the rebels. Yet, though they hanged and tortured, neither king, judge nor lords could kill the spirit of the people. Face to face with their enemies, they neither cringed nor begged for mercy, despite the knowledge that a horrible death awaited them. They went to their death as proudly as they had fought. Of most of them, from the leaders to the humblest of the rank and file, the same story is told. John Starling, who did not deny that he had executed the Archbishop, was sentenced to death. Before his death, he said that he was a proud man to have been able to execute the traitor Archbishop.

In St. Albans, William Grindcobbe awaited his trial. Despite the courageous stand of the townsfolk, he had been arrested by a trick of Tressilian. When the King's Council declared that it intended to send troops to St. Albans, Sir Walter Atte Lee, who came from those parts, declared to the king that he could arrest Grindcobbe without a battle with the people of St. Albans.

A rumour was spread that the king and his army were approaching St. Albans. When the people heard this, they grew alarmed. But Grindcobbe cheered them:

> "Be of good heart," he said, "for we are well provided; help will not be wanting for us, as long as our money shall not fail. See, the towns around us are in alliance with us, and they will come to our help if need be. Let us ride forth tomorrow like men, to meet the knights outside the town, and let us ask, before they get near to our town, whether their coming is in peace. And if not, we will drive them from our town with blows."

This fighting speech put fresh courage into the people, but when they rode out they met Atte Lee, instead of the king's forces. In a speech to them, Atte Lee told them he came as their friend, that it was best for them to surrender to the king, for he had so great an army with him "for miles around no fodder nor any corn, no fruits of the earth, fresh or old are left, but all things are consumed and trodden down". It was in order to prevent this from happening that he, Atte Lee, had told the king that he would see that all was peacefully settled. "As a neighbour and friend" he asked that the leaders should be handed over to him, and that all which had been taken from the Abbot should be returned to him including the charters he had surrendered. Upon the conclusion of his speech, he selected twelve townsmen and empanelled them as a jury, asking them to indict the most guilty leaders. But when he summoned the jury, their reply soon made him realise that his scheme was not going to proceed as smoothly as he had hoped. They said that:

> "they could indict none, could charge no one; that all were good and faithful men of the king and they knew none else amongst them."

The jury considered that the actions of their fellow townsmen were fully justified, for they were carrying out the will of the king.

After long negotiations which resulted in deadlock, Walter Atte Lee decided to throw diplomacy to the winds and proceed by force. Secretly calling together some bailiffs and retainers of the Abbot, men whom he could trust, he ordered them to arrest the three most notorious leaders at dead of night and immediately to take them to Hertford, where he would be waiting. The orders were carried out and the arrested men were imprisoned in Hertford jail, closely guarded by armed men.

When the arrests became known, fresh fighting broke out in St. Albans. A group of responsible townsmen was sent to Hertford to obtain the release of Grindcobbe. He was released, but under pledge that he would use his influence to restore the charter to the Abbot. The delegation from St. Albans was also informed that, unless these charters were restored, Grindcobbe would be executed.

When this was told to the people of St. Albans, they demanded that the charters should be restored to the Abbot in order that Grindcobbe's life might be saved. But Grindcobbe refused to do this. To the assembled people of St. Albans, he made a speech which, although reported by Walsingham, the hostile chronicler of St. Albans, after 600 years, still brings to us the breath of his magnificent spirit:

> "Fellow citizens, your new born liberty has at last removed the burden of an age long tyranny. Stand firm now while you may; lose no courage because of the penalty to be inflicted on me. I am to die for that liberty which we have won. But if I fall, I shall think myself happy to end my life as a martyr for such a cause. Act now as you would have acted had my head been struck off in Hertford yesterday."

This speech fired the blood of the listeners. They swore to defend their liberties and reproached themselves bitterly for not beheading Atte Lee when they had him in their hands. But nothing could be done. Tressilian and his troops had by now arrived, and had tricked an unwitting jury into indicting Grindcobbe and others by telling them that these men had already been indicted by another jury. To prove this he showed them an indictment referring to cases which had already been tried in other areas. Believing Tressilian, and being unable to read, the jury drew up the indictment.

Grindcobbe, with fifteen others who had taken an active part in the rising, were hanged and drawn. By special order of the king, they were to be left swinging on the gibbet "for as long as they could last". But they were too well loved by the people to be allowed to hang in such a manner, and not be granted the peace of the grave. Their bodies were cut down and buried secretly, but their corpses were not allowed to rest. The graves were traced and, by command of the king, the bodies were exhumed and re-hanged on the gibbet.

Thomas Walsingham describes how the citizens were forced to hang the corpses in dogs' chains:

> "This command (of the king) turned the villeins of St. Albans, who were still rebelling for freedom, into slaves of a vile and horrible servitude. Whilst, not having anyone who

would be willing to do such a service for them, they were obliged with their own hands to hang their fellow citizens again in iron chains; and by now their bodies diffused with corruption, swarming with vermin, rotten and stinking, gave forth to them a most revolting smell. And indeed this was deservedly the foul office of the men who unjustly took upon themselves the name of citizens; by this deed bringing upon themselves a lasting reproach, which shall not be removed; And those who preferred to conceal and falsify truth, rather than to betray such traitors to us, were not for nothing obliged to hand them themselves. Dogs too followed them because they did not deserve to be lords!

"Because, forsooth, it was as though, in the judgment of God, the forsworn and the rebellious, hateful to God, were proved to be worse than dogs while, their dogs being set free, they were bound themselves to the service of so execrable a servitude."[1]

But Tressilian had not yet finished. Before him at St. Albans stood John Ball. He had been arrested in Coventry and was brought to trial on July 13. He, too, faced the court for the last time in the same spirit as he had faced that whole hated class for so many years. This was the end. He and his beloved people had tried and failed. Perhaps, in later years, others might again sound the bell which he and Wat Tyler had rung but which was now silent. He had been near enough to see the promised land for which he had been ceaselessly working for the greater part of his life, but he was not to enter it. Perhaps others following would learn from his mistakes, would learn that the common people should put their trust neither in kings nor in princes, but only in themselves.

In return for the mercy they had shown, for they had executed only those deemed to be traitors to the commons of

[1] Walsingham's account of the hanging is a fitting postscript to the king's speech to the Essex rebels. Three hundred years later a similar act of indignity was performed by the ruling class on the corpse of Oliver Cromwell.

England, they were to be exterminated. They had executed quickly those traitors who had brought ruin, hunger and misery to England, executed them quickly after a brief trial. But the leaders of the commons were to have no such grace. They were to be hanged, drawn and quartered.

Fearlessly, John Ball answered the questions of Justice Tressilian. Yes, he had played a leading part in the rebellion. Yes, they were his letters, written by him and sent out as instructions to the people. No, he did not consider his acts as blameworthy for he believed in all he had written, said and done; he would withdraw nothing and could repent nothing. Thereupon he was sentenced to be hanged, drawn, beheaded and quartered, but at the intercession of the Bishop of London, Tressilian allowed John Ball two days' respite. The Bishop was anxious for the soul of John Ball and wanted two days' grace for Ball's repentance.

So, on July 15, 1381, at St. Albans, facing the king and his court to the last, the great English rebel mounted to the scaffold. Judgement was carried out to the full letter of the law, and his quartered body was sent to the four corners of England and there exposed as a warning to the commons of England.

One day later, on July 16, John Shirle was arrested at Cambridge. Shirle was one of the "messengers" who claimed membership of a "Great Society". He had until July 15 evaded arrest, but the news of the death of Ball was too much for him. He could not keep silent. He was charged with holding a meeting in a Cambridge tavern where he told those assembled—and there were many—how Ball had died. Shirle told his audience the things for which Ball had stood, what a true and honest man he was and how hard he had fought for the commons. He went on to say that the king's ministers and officials should have suffered Ball's fate and that it would not be long before Ball's death was avenged.

Like other rebels, Shirle maintained his defiant attitude when on trial. He made no attempt to deny that he had spoken these words, and was sentenced to death.

Two others, John Wright and George Dunsby, were charged with carrying incendiary messages from the "Great Society" throughout Norfolk. Whilst proceeding to the scaffold, they too declared that they were proud of their work and were glad to have been able to serve the commons faithfully.

Meanwhile the rising in East Anglia had been ruthlessly crushed, mainly by the action of Henry Spencer, Bishop of Norwich. Henry was a fighting man, descended from fighting men, and certainly showed, during his vigorous suppression of the rising, that he was more expert in the art of slaying than of saving. Henry, however, was true to his cloth and was careful of the health of those he slaughtered and often confessed his victims before their death. "To those who were killed in battle, the bishop's sword brought absolution", exulted a monk. Never had the church sought so zealously, not even for its dues and tithes, as did the Bishop for rebels. From Peterborough to Ramsey, from Ramsey to Cambridge, and from Cambridge to Newmarket, rode the bishop, banishing peace and bringing the sword. Near Icklingham he encountered the men sent by Litster to the king, to ask for further charters. The bishop, after questioning the knights, hanged the three peasants and freed the others. The fighting bishop then rode on to Norwich, which had already been evacuated by Litster, who had decided to muster reinforcements and face the bishop's force, which by now had grown to a considerable size.

Litster made his last stand at North Walsham. Deploying his forces in the same dispositions as the men of Essex, he stood awaiting the bishop. He had not long to wait, for as soon as the bishop saw Litster's forces he ordered a cavalry charge. With himself in the van, the cavalry smashed through the defences and slaughtered to their hearts' content. The bishop went berserk. So out of control was he that "he foamed at the mouth like a wild boar", as he slew the rebels with his two-edged sword.[1]

Litster was captured and tried by the bishop. He, too, was sentenced to the same fate as John Ball. Having condemned Litster, the bishop confessed and absolved him and, as he was being dragged on a hurdle towards the gallows, the bishop raised Litster's head lest it should be hurt against the stones in the road. One quarter of the mutilated body was sent to Norwich, and hung from the house which had been his headquarters. Another was sent to Harwich, a third to Yarmouth and the fourth to Lynn, so that "rebels and insurgents against the peace might learn by what end they will finish their careers".

So far as is known John Wrawe was the only rebel leader to turn informer. During his trial he turned king's evidence, and drew up a list indicting all who had participated with him in the rising. As is usual with such men, he put the entire blame upon the others. But his act of treachery did not absolve his guilt in the eyes of his judges for, although the king's peace was extended to him, he was hanged in June 1382. It says much for a movement that it produced men like Shirle, Grindcobbe, and John Ball, but only one Wrawe.

Kent offered as desperate a resistance as Essex. It took three months to pacify that county. At the end of August, the Earl of Kent—who seems to have recovered his nerve after his escape over the fields of Whitechapel—having inspected the villages, deemed it safe for the king and his Council to visit the county. Richard came, and doubtless duly ad-

[1] It should be added that the bishop's fearless valour was only shown against badly armed peasants. When in 1383 he led his notorious crusade to Flanders and came up against an armed feudal force, he was utterly defeated.

mired the gallows fruit hanging from the gibbets in the garden county. Yet the chatter of his courtiers had scarcely died away from between the rows of gallows before rebellion again broke out.

On September 29, 1381, a large force of rebels attacked and captured Maidstone, arrested the sheriff and some other gentlemen, and put them to death. From Maidstone, the rebels marched to Deptford but the impetus could carry them no further. It was an isolated act of despair, for it had neither the leadership nor the force to succeed. The rising was suppressed, but not before it had shown a significant change in the outlook of the peasants. The rebels demanded the ratification of the charters presented to them at Mile End. If this was refused, then the court *and the king* would be put to death. Shirle too had threatened the king with death in his speech at the inn. They had lost confidence in Richard, but not in the office of kingship because, although the rebels now intended to kill Richard, they proposed to place John of Gaunt on the throne in his place. Gaunt had remained on the Scottish border throughout the rising and although he had been detailed to crush the rising in Yorkshire, nevertheless, because his hands were relatively free from the excesses of the others and because he was not involved in the machiavellian policy of the King's Council, the remainder of the rebels had turned in his favour and gave him their support.

Most of the well born and wealthy who had joined the rebels were imprisoned and not put to death. Farringdon was issued with letters of grace on March 8, 1382, whilst after a long-drawn-out process, Sybyle, Carlyll and Tonge were released on surety of £300 each, fifteen days after Easter, 1383, because the court could not find enough evidence. They refused to benefit from an amnesty of November, 1381, because that implied guilt, and in 1384 they were completely acquitted for lack of witnesses. Sir Roger Bacon was for a short time imprisoned in the Tower, and also released. Robert Cave, the baker of Dartford, was neither well born nor wealthy, and was sentenced to ten years imprisonment.[1]

Most of the more bloody acts of repression took place immediately after the rising had been suppressed. Judging by medieval standards the reprisals were moderate. Indeed the number of pardons which was issued was extraordinary. Trial by jury was continued all the time (after the first acts of reprisal) and the pursuit of the rebels was soon over.

This holding back of large-scale reprisals was not due to a liberal attitude towards the rebel peasants. That was not a medieval virtue The chief reason why moderate counsel soon prevailed was that the ruling class were afraid to go in for such widespread slaughter no matter how much they desired it. They were too insecure. The peasants were still a formidable force and still an uncertain factor; their fighting spirit was still there, as was seen by the stands made and the rear-guard actions fought. Furthermore there was the labour problem. The Black Death had removed many peasants. What was to happen to the fields if thousands more serfs were slain? What effect would it have on the economic life of the country? Consequently the brake was applied and a general pardon was proclaimed by Parliament on November 13, 1381, It did not, however, cover 287 of the more active insurgents who had evaded capture, nor did it include those towns which had so whole-heartedly joined in the risings. It was some time before Bury St. Edmunds, Cambridge, Scarborough, Bridgwater and other places, were deemed to have reached a state of grace and could be included in the comity of English cities and towns.

Gradually life assumed its normal course. The ruling class

1 An echo of Walsingham's attitude towards the rebels is reflected in Professor Oman's comment on this sentence. He writes: "Considering the sanitary condition of medieval prisons we must conclude that he possessed a wonderful constitution."

slid back into its accustomed place, on the shoulders of the peasants, the position from which it had been so violently thrust. Now God is in his heaven; the baron is in his castle; and the serf is back in his hut. "Law and Order" reign supreme.

CHAPTER TWELVE

# AFTERMATH

THE PEASANTS in 1381 suffered a crushing defeat, though, as we shall show, this and other agrarian revolts were important causes of the collapse of the feudal order.

A peasant victory, in the sense of a durable transfer of power to the peasants as a class, was in fact impossible, then as always. The peasantry cannot, and never has, become a ruling class. This fact is simply explained by the character of the peasant economy.

First of all, since the peasants are petty commodity producers in a primitive agrarian society, they are dispersed, not concentrated. The focus of their existence is the village or hamlet where they must remain at all times, supervising the routine of agricultural life, husbanding the meagre surplus from the year's work which a slight change in climatic or market conditions may eliminate in the following year.

Secondly, because of their dispersal and the precarious character of their existence, they are economically at the mercy of the merchant and usurer, and therefore politically impotent. Even were they to kill every lord in the kingdom, the peasant would still be dependent on dealers in grain and livestock for contact with all but immediately local consumers. Merchant and usurer were often one and the same person. The peasant whose crop had failed, or whose beasts of burden had died of the murrain, had to turn to anyone who possessed liquid wealth in order to survive. It was to the tune often of several hundred, never less than fifty per cent, that he became the dependant of the money-lender.

The richest peasants of the village often increased their income by usury. Here we are in the presence of another phenomenon which made peasant rule impossible. This was a class which was in a constant flux. Petty commodity production in agriculture as in industry constantly throws up small capitalists, and at the other end of the scale depresses the unfortunate into propertyless wage-earners. Owing to the low development of production for the market, and the decline in population in the fourteenth and fifteenth centuries, as compared with two centuries later, this process was not sufficiently advanced completely to disrupt the village community—or the temporary political unity of the peasantry. But it had begun as has already been shown. The rich peasants after 1381 provided a source of recruitment to the gentry, as did the gentry to the nobility. Had the existing nobility been eliminated, it would have been replaced as a result of this constant movement of social differentiation among the agricultural producers by another nobility—or by a completely new class, the bourgeoisie, bringing with it a new mode of production. As a matter of fact, the old nobility very soon eliminated itself. It was replaced by a new nobility, whose triumph was, however, shortlived, for the conditions out of which it arose also generated the capitalist mode of production and the bourgeois class.

State power in the hands of the peasants themselves was therefore inconceivable, and there was no element in society which could represent the interests of the peasants. The artisans were numerically too few, and in any case had interests (as urban consumers) which conflicted with those of the peasants. Merchants were in different ways exploiters of the peasants. The peasants, as the story of the revolt shows, clearly recognised who were their exploiters and their enemies—but for one. That was the king. Their seemingly inexplicable trust in the contemptible Richard was not, however, simple folly. It was an unconscious recognition on their part that they could not create a state of their own. Although they envisaged a popular monarchy, it was still a monarchy, and they obviously thought of the king as wielding executive power on their behalf.

Their illusion about the monarchy may well have had deep historical roots. They may have preserved in some way memories of the age of the tribal monarchies, when kings and nobles were hardly distinguishable from the freemen of the tribe, except by the greater honour and voluntary tribute accorded to warrior leaders. More important, the state power in the feudal epoch, as in other forms of class society including our own, was presented as an impartial force hovering above, and reconciling, the conflicting interests of society. The king was said to be the source of all law, the lion of justice, punisher of wrong-doers and protector of the weak. Because he was frequently obliged to suppress discordant elements within the ruling class, in the general interests of that class, the illusion of his impartiality as between rulers and ruled was strengthened. But if that illusion disappeared when the king appeared openly as the leader of the forces of oppression, it was always too late, for by then the revolt was as good as crushed.

So the rising was repressed, but neither the first bloody suppression of the rising, nor the more politic amnesty that followed, removed the fundamental causes of the revolt. It is true that not until the English Revolution of 1640 to 1649 was the whole structure of the state so seriously attacked as in 1381. But during the two and a half centuries intervening, disintegrating feudal society was wracked by intermittent agrarian revolt and civil war, necessary conditions for its eventual destruction. The wave of revolt which reached its peak in 1381 did not subside immediately. The official records provide evidence of a continuation after 1381 of the sporadic village revolts which had been so frequent in the period preceding the Great Revolt. There was even a plan for another large-scale rising in 1382 in East Anglia, and yet another in 1384 in Sussex. Both these projects were based on the programme of 1381. But both were scotched, the one as a result of betrayal before it was launched, the other in its early stages.

We have already seen that the social struggles over the appropriation of rent had by 1381 become much more complex than a simple defence by the peasantry of its standard of life. The peasant struggle against feudalism was beginning to contain elements of the struggle of an as yet embryo class of small capitalists against feudal restrictions. This element becomes more significant in the fifteenth and sixteenth centuries and eventually part of the movement becomes antagonistic to the struggle of the poorer peasants for decent conditions of existence. The Lollard movement of the early fifteenth century, led by a section of the country gentry, was in form a religious movement but it had a deeper social meaning. It should be regarded as the remote ancestor of seventeenth-century Puritanism, not only in its religious aspects, but as a movement of the gentry, the heralds of small capitalism. Lollardry was suppressed though not eliminated. But social revolt continued. A combination of peasant discontent, hatred of a corrupt government and political criticism led to the very considerable uprising of the commons of Kent under Jack Cade in 1450. This too must be regarded as the continuation rather of the embryo capitalist forms present in the movement of 1381, than as simply a peasant protest against feudal oppression.

There used to be a somewhat sterile debate between historians of the fifteenth century as to whether the conditions of the people, in particular the peasantry, had improved or deteriorated during the period. The historians concerned had little appreciation either of the class forces involved, or of the character of social and economic change during the period of the decline of a historical epoch such as feudalism, and neither view gets to the root of the matter. In fact, the general collapse of the mode of production which we call feudal did lead to all the symptoms of economic and political decay which are characteristic of a dying social order. The crisis of the private and public revenues of the feudal nobility continued. But within the old order the new forces of society, most especially in the country districts, continued to grow. The peasantry, due in no small part to their readiness to revolt, were winning the battle for rent. In so doing the social differentiation within their ranks continued apace, especially in districts where the richer peasants were also able to take part in the domestic production of woollen cloth, in which England was becoming pre-eminent in Europe.

It is the development of capitalist forms in agriculture, associated especially with the development of the cloth industry, which complicates the fierce agrarian struggles of the sixteenth century. Most of these revolts, of which that of Ket in 1549 is an outstanding example, were to a considerable extent directed against the enclosure movement. Many of the medium-sized capitalist farmers of yeoman or gentry origin were enclosing arable land piecemeal so as to convert to sheep pasture. This process went ahead at first without arousing much opposition. But when some of the nobility and the rich city merchants who had bought up manors in the country started to cash in on the high profits to be made in wool production, trouble began. These individuals enclosed whole villages, especially in the Midlands, and evicted all the arable peasant farmers from their holdings. This episode in the process of the primitive accumulation of capital had the partial effect of dividing the peasantry from some of the capitalist opponents of feudal restrictions on production. But the story cannot be told adequately without a consideration of the political factors involved, which is beyond the scope of this work.

It is, however, appropriate to point to some of the political aspects of the disintegration of the feudal order. These are as significant as, and indeed inseparable from, the underlying economic developments which were beginning to disrupt society in 1381 and which continued to do so in the centuries following. The fifteenth century is notorious as an age of civil war. Almost as soon as the peasants had been defeated in 1381, the faction fights among the nobles were renewed with a ferocity unparalleled even in the reign of Edward II, culminating in 1399 with the deposition and murder of Richard II by his cousin, Henry Bolingbroke, Earl of Derby, son of John of Gaunt. This victory of the Lancastrians did not result in a healing of the breach between factions. Bolingbroke's rule as Henry IV was punctuated by feudal risings, and the internecine war was only temporarily assuaged by Henry V's predatory and eventually disastrous war against France.

By the middle of the century the divisions among the nobles seemed irreconcilable. Although neither the peasants nor the townsfolk threw in their lot with either section of their oppressors within the nobility, the political divisions went very deep. The evils associated with the system of indenture for life-time service with a great magnate, already (as mentioned above) present in the middle of the fourteenth century, were multiplied. A reign of terror affected every county. Great nobles aligned themselves with York or Lancaster as much in conformity with their interests in local politics as because of ties with the leaders of the factions. Lesser nobles and some of the yeomen were tied by fear, cupidity and hate to one or other of the retinues of the contending barons, earls and dukes. Bands of armed men occupied their enemies' village and collected the peasants' rents before the legal owner's steward came along for the same purpose. False charges were framed, and those who were the enemies of the faction which had control of local administration, were dragged up for trial by juries empanelled by their opponents. Feudal order was dissolving into anarchy, and there seems little reason to doubt that the root cause was that the rulers of feudal society were quarrelling over the diminishing returns of their system.

The victories of the Yorkist faction in 1461, and of the Tudor branch of the house of Lancaster in 1485 were both the cause and effect of the concentration of feudal factionalism and eventually of feudal power. The Yorkists and Tudors won because in the fight more of their opponents than of their allies were liquidated. And of course they used the control of the state machine, which they achieved with victory, to liquidate the remnants of the opposition. The Tudor absolutism, sometimes represented as a new, anti-feudal form of state, was in fact a state representing the dynasty which managed to centralise all feudal power and all feudal rights into its own hand. This was the culmination of a political process which had begun as early as the end of the thirteenth century. The impotence of state power at various periods during the fourteenth and fifteenth centuries seems to contradict this conception of a long period of development of feudal absolutism, though this occasional impotence did in fact make the establishment of a powerful centralisation easier.

Above all it must be remembered that the faction battles and victories of the noble parties and their kings were not the only causes of the developing absolutism. Both the early and later stages of absolutism were inseparable from the means taken to suppress peasant revolt. The fourteenth-century Justices of Labourers and the sixteenth-century Justices of the Peace had similar functions—to preserve the social fabric. At both periods these unpaid representatives of the state machine did their job with zeal and if necessary ferocity. But the feudal state was eventually hoist with its own petard.

The centralised monarchy which was the result of the elimination of the feudal rivals of the Tudors favoured the growth of urban and rural capitalism, in spite of the restrictive policy of the government. This development of capitalism in agriculture, industry and trade is the most important historical event in sixteenth and seventeenth century England, for it created a class of country gentry and merchants who by 1640 were prepared not to defend but to smash the bankrupt absolutist state and to put in its place something in their own image.

## *SUGGESTIONS FOR FURTHER READING*

This is not meant to be an exhaustive bibliography, but an indication to the reader who wants to pursue further his investigations into the subject matter of this book, as to what should be the first steps.

### PART I.

*Chapter I.* The analysis of the nature of feudal society and its crisis derives much from the writings of Karl Marx and V. I. Lenin. Most important (leaving aside the question of the general theoretical approach) are Chapters XX and XLVII of Vol. III of *Capital,* entitled respectively "Historical Data Concerning Merchant's Capital" and "The Genesis of Capitalist Ground Rent". Lenin's writings on the agrarian question will be found in Volumes I and XII of the *Selected Works.* M. H. Dobb's *Studies in the Development of Capitalism* is essential for the further understanding of these works of Marx and Lenin. A very good short general survey of English feudal society is M. Gibbs's *Feudal Order.*

Still the best books in English on the agrarian structure of medieval England are those of Paul Vinogradoff. The most useful are *The Growth of the Manor* and *Villeinage in England.* Useful material will also be found in G. C. Homan's *English Villagers of the Thirteenth Century.* Much inferior as a picture of medieval village life is H. S. Bennett's *Life on the English Manor 1100-1400.* A good account of the economy and administration of a great medieval estate is R. A. L. Smith's *Canterbury Cathedral Priory.* The features of the collapse of the feudal estate are discussed in the first three chapters of R. H. Tawney's *Agrarian Problem in the Sixteenth Century;* A. E. Levett's *Studies in Manorial History;* M. Morgan's *English Lands of the Abbey of Bec;* and R. H. Hilton's *Economic Development of Some Leicestershire Estates.* Important articles on this theme are by the Soviet historian, E. A. Kosminsky, "Services and Money Rents in the Thirteenth Century" in *Economic History Review,* 1935; and by M. M. Postan, "The Chronology of Labour Services", *Transactions of the Royal Historical Society,* Fourth Series, XX.

An extremely solid, if dry book on the Statute of Labourers is *The Enforcement of the Statute of Labourers,* by B. Putnam. Much of the evidence on which a portion of this chapter is based is cited in an article by R. H. Hilton, "Peasant Movements in England Before 1381", in *Economic History Review,* 1949. An interesting and readable book on the wool trade is E. Power's *Medieval English Wool Trade.* There is no comparable work on the cloth industry, but some information will be found in E. Lipson's *Economic History of England,* Vol. I, and his *History of the English Woollen and Worsted Industries.* Dobb's book, cited above, should be read as a corrective to Lipson. Useful articles on the European background to English agrarian and industrial history will be found in *Cambridge Economic History,* Vols. I and II, and E. Power's article, "Peasant Life and Agrarian Conditions", in *Cambridge Medieval History,* Vol. VII, gives a short account covering most European countries.

*Chapter II.* The best historian of industry and commerce is George Unwin, whose *Gilds and Companies of London, Finance and Trade Under Edward III,* and the earlier chapters of *Industrial Organisation in the Sixteenth and Seventeenth Centuries,* deal with problems raised in this chapter. The recent *Merchant Class of Medieval London,* by Sylvia Thrupp, is full of material, but is inferior in analysis. Mrs. J. R. Green's *Town Life in the Fifteenth Century* (two vols.), though containing many unacceptable interpretations, is also full of useful information. M. D. Lobel's *Borough of Bury St. Edmunds* is a good short history. The much older *Life in an Old English Town,* by M. Dormer Harris, is a first-rate account of social and political struggles in medieval Coventry, giving a good insight into the problems of a typical town of the time.

There is no good general history of Edward III's reign. The following works will give information on different aspects of the period. There are short factual articles in the *Cambridge Medieval History,* Vol. VII. Though old and modified in many respects by later research, W. Stubbs's *Constitutional History of England* is still worth reading. It contains, along with other material, a political narrative. So does T. F. Tout's *Chapters in Medieval Administrative History,* Vol. III, which is also essential for a study of the state machinery during the period. A modern work is J. E. A. Joliffe's *Constitutional History of Medieval England*. J. Armitage Smith's *John of Gaunt* is a useful biography. The best short history of the Hundred Years' War, emphasising equally French and English history, is the French historian, E. Perroy's *Guerre de Cent Ans,* which is being translated into English. There is an excellent detailed summary of the political situation in England on the eve of the rising in A. Steele's *Richard II.*

*Chapter III.* Useful introductory works on the church in the fourteenth century are D. Knowles's *The Religious Orders in England* (a Catholic work), which is very readable, and A. Hamilton Thompson's *English Clergy in the Later Middle Ages,* which is less so. Medieval political theories are described in the six volumes of *Medieval Political Theory in the West,* by R. W. and A. J. Carlyle, and in one volume in C. H. McIlwain's *Growth of Political Thought in the West.* Still worthwhile reading are essays by R. L. Poole in his *Illustrations in the History of Medieval Thought.* H. Rashdall's *Universities of Europe in the Middle Ages* (ed. Powicke and Emden) is a comprehensive account of medieval universities and their curricula. The most accessible guide (no more) to English literature in the period is the *Cambridge History of English Literature,* but Chaucer should be read in the original, e.g. in Skeat's *The Students' Chaucer* (a complete edition). Froissart and Langland can be read in the modernised versions in the Everyman Library.

S. Painter's *Studies in the History of the English Feudal Baronage* summarises recent work on feudal institutions to the end of the thirteenth century. Pollock and Maitland's *History of English Law* is an essential reference book for the same period, covering much wider ground than is suggested by the title. J. Huizinga's *Waning of the Middle Ages* is a survey, mainly from literary sources, of the decay of medieval civilisation in Europe.

*Chapter IV.* G. Barraclough's *Papal Provisions* is the best guide to the subject. Both scholarly and readable is H. B. Workman's *John Wyclif* (two vols.). A vast amount of material from medieval (especially fourteenth century) sermons is described and quoted in G. R. Owst's *Preaching in Medieval England* and *Literature and Pulpit in Medieval England.* Political verses of the period are collected by T. Wright in *Political Songs* (Camden Society) and *Political Poems and Songs* (Rolls Series). A vast collection of ballads, including those featuring Robin Hood, is F. J. Childe's *English and Scottish Ballads.*

## PART TWO

Only the most important and authoritative works on the actual rising will be mentioned here. The best and most detailed is unfortunately in French, *Le Soulèvement des Travailleurs d'Angleterre en 1381,* by A. Réville and C. Petit-Dutaillis. There is a short discussion by the latter on some points in his *Studies and Notes Supplementary to Stubbs's Constitutional History,* Vol. II. G. M. Trevelyan's *England in the Age of Wycliffe* is pleasantly written, but completely outmoded by recent research. His *Social History of England* is hardly more up-to-date. E. Powell's *Rising in East Anglia in 1381* is a detailed regional study (duplicating to some extent the work of Réville). Sir Charles Oman's *Great Revolt of 1381* is a useful storehouse of facts and references, but is written from a standpoint even more hostile to and contemptuous of the rebels than those already quoted. A more sympathetic attitude is that of A. Steele in a chapter on the rising in the work cited above.

Of specialist articles about the rising, the most useful for those beginning the study of the period are G. Kriehn's "Studies in the Sources of the Social Revolt in 1381" in the *American Historical Review,* 1902, and B. Wilkinson's "Peasants' Revolt of 1381" in *Speculum,* 1940. Most of the contemporary chronicle material is in Latin or French, and is therefore beyond the reach of the average reader. The English version of Froissart's *Chronicles of France, England and Spain* has been mentioned. Also in English is the work of the sixteenth-century historian, John Stow. His *Annales of England* should not, of course, be regarded in the same way as the writings of contemporaries, but he embodies in almost literal translation much from chroniclers contemporary with the rising, and some material not now known. His fascinating *Survey of London,* which is full of historical allusions, is published in the Everyman Library.

# INDEX